Mary, Come Home!

Mary, Come Home!

Mary A. Bullis

BROADMAN PRESS
Nashville, Tennessee

4263-30
ISBN: 0-8054-6330-5

Dewey Decimal Classification: 266.092
Subject headings: BULLIS, MARY A. / / MISSIONS HOME

Library of Congress Catalog Card Number: 82-71445
Printed in the United States of America

Contents

Introduction   7

1 Mary, Come Home!   9

2 Rejections   12

3 "Tryouts"   16

4 Dilemma in My First Pioneer Mission Field   21

5 My Boastful Friend   24

6 My Father's Eyes   28

7 Mountains to Possess   33

8 Vacation Plus   37

9 A Tribute to Pioneer Pastors' Children   40

10 Giants in Our Land   43

11 The Leader of Many   46

12 Rock of Gibraltar   49

13 My Dear Pixie   52

14 Tim's Greatest Undeserved Punishment   55

15 God's Unfailing Clock   58

16 Death in the Parsonage   66

17 Sharp Stones and Rock Pillows   72

18 Glad Tidings of Good Things   80

19 Open House   85

20 God's Protection   88

21 The Big End of the Stick   95

22 The Computer's Choice?   99

23 The Crossing Over   103

24 Thy Will Be Done   108

Epilogue   114

IN MEMORIAM
Mary Alice Bullis

Little did we realize that our wife and mother would hear "Mary, come home!" from her Lord only a few weeks before the release of her book, *Mary, Come Home!* Now we look forward all the more to "that blessed hope, and the glorious appearing of the great God and our Saviour Jesus Christ" (Titus 2:13), when the entire Bullis family will be at home with Mary.

Ten and a half months before Jesus called her home, the kids bought her a gloxinia plant for her sickroom. Later the blooms fell off, leaving only the green leaves. On the very day Mary left us, we looked at the plant through tear-filled eyes. It had bloomed again!

She "being dead yet speaketh" (Heb. 11:4).

JIM BULLIS
On behalf of VIRGINIA,
BOB, DARYL, DAVE, and
TIM BULLIS

Introduction

God in his great wisdom knows my comings and my goings from the time I was conceived until the last throb of my heart. My wisdom is so minuscule, like a tiny speck of light. I see only a few steps ahead of me.

Long ago, my husband Jim and I searched a United States map and the Southern Baptist college catalogs. Our youthful eighteen years of "wisdom" allowed us to set a course only for the next few months. As "half adult" we planned to strike out for new horizons. Placing a finger on my home in Saint Louis, Missouri, and on Denver, Colorado, where Jim's parents were living, we found Howard Payne College in Brownwood, Texas, to be an equal distance from both.

Our "wisdom" knew only miles, while God's wisdom encompassed the future. This included two rejections by the Foreign Mission Board; pioneer missions in Ohio; opening new areas in Western New York; and later the crossing of the Niagara River into beautiful Ontario, Canada.

His eyes foresaw nine chapels beginning; "Sno Kone" evangelism transforming Bible Schools over a large area; and more than eleven thousand children enrolled in Bible Schools through one church in nine years. It included New York's first Southern Baptist "church-owned" day-camp land; two day-care center programs; and the first-known bus ministry in a Southern Baptist church in the New York Convention.

God's direction led us to cross into Ontario, Canada, where we found a new fertile field for Southern Baptists. An estimated two percent of the population is Baptist.

If God's wisdom had allowed us to see his whole plan for our lives, we would have been frightened. But because he allowed us to see it step by step, it gave our faith time to grow into more faith and then extra faith (Rom. 1:17).

Throughout I have used a series of questions to introduce thoughts about our faith and its various stages of growth. May the answers from the Lord add to your faith in the Father's daily care.

1
——Mary, Come Home!——

DEAR DAUGHTER:

Mary, why don't you come home? Jim and you have worked hard at starting churches. You need to slow down because of your health. It may be time to come back to Missouri where Jim can pastor an ordinary church. We would help you relocate back home.

Love,

Daddy

As I read the note from my father, Arnold Epps, it seemed such a long time since our hands had been held tightly, as we planned our move away from home. We planned to be married and make our college home in Brownwood, Texas. We wanted to be independent, and this college was a thousand miles from both parents.

Jim had just arrived to get his blood test. He admitted he had never sought my father's permission. On the day before the wedding he found my father alone. Jim summoned his courage and asked the question. My father laughed at Jim's awkwardness and said, "The wedding is tomorrow. The cake is baked; the flowers are coming; it is a little late for me to disapprove." I was thankful my parents had trusted me to Jim's company. Someone asked my father if he worried about my leaving home and going so far away. His answer was, "Not as long as she is with Jim."

Three years before, Jim had started attending my church. He grew rapidly as a Christian. This growth helped him make a public commitment for lifetime Christian service.

I remember we had been friends in both church and high school Bible

9

club. Our first date had come after a beautiful experience. Our Sunday
School department was to have its Valentine coronation. Two chairs
were placed in the front, one for the king and one for the queen. The
royal robes and crowns were ready.

The pages, with scepters in their hands, started in two directions.
One came to my side and tapped me. I was taken to be robed and
crowned. The second page returned with the king. It was Jim. He was
seated at my side. I looked at him and knew it was an eventful evening.
After the coronation was over, Jim asked to take me home. The queen
could only do the king's bidding. From that moment the king courted
the queen.

As a young child, I had prayed, "Father, if you want me to be a
missionary, I am willing." After going with Jim for a time, I realized
his lifetime commitment was not as a foreign missionary. He planned to
be a preacher.

A young man had come to our church. This mission volunteer was
interested in me. This new development confused me. What if God had
planned for me to be a missionary, and Jim was wrong for me? I shared
this fear with a friend, who prayed with me for God's leadership. I
prayed, "Oh, Father, if Jim is the one I am to marry, help him to ask me
one more time."

The next morning we were getting ready for church. Deacon Epps
had made it a family rule to be the first at church. I made everyone late
this Sunday morning. Mother said, "Mary, you will be late for your
wedding!" Her words made me think of my prayer.

At church Jim drove up and parked his car. He came silently across
the street. He didn't say hello or good morning. No word did he speak
until he was standing in front of me. Then, only five words, "Mary, will
you marry me?"

"Oh, yes," I said. And silently to the Father I thought, *Thank you for
answering my prayer. I will be the best pastor's wife I can be.*

Our lives during the next twenty-eight years would be further proof
of God's selection. I knew there could be only one answer to my father's
letter. Neither sickness nor health, poverty nor abundance, hardships
nor comforts had any bearing on what we would do until death separates
us from our task.

My parents had always backed us up in our mission ventures. Their
small monthly check over the years was a concrete example of their

support. This letter was voicing their concern for my physical well-being. I knew we would have no problem finding a church in Ohio, Missouri, or other parts of the United States.

At peace, I picked up my pen and wrote to my Father:

> DEAR DADDY:
> I cannot come home. Jim and I saw another beautiful garden. The countryside is well kept. Our neighbor, Canada, has so few Baptists, but no Southern Baptist reapers are to be found in the "Golden Horseshoe" area of Ontario.
> Thank you for your concern which has been evident through the years.
>
> Your Daughter,
>
> Mary

O Father, thank you for making me daughter, wife, and servant in such beautiful gardens.

2
————Rejections————

Watching the small, creeping hands of the clock made the day seem long. We were waiting for the telephone to ring.

When it did ring, our breathing slowed. "Was it . . . ?"

We found it was a friend, a church member, or a neighbor eager to hear the news.

The large and small hands of the clock tied in their ceaseless race. At 4:20 PM the telephone started its short song. It only released one note from its throat before Jim's hand prevented the second.

"Hello? . . . Yes, we know the Foreign Mission Board met today."

As I watched his face during the heavy silence on our end of the line, I knew we were not going to Colombia, South America.

My thoughts went back to the age of twelve when I spent many evenings reading a few Scripture verses over and over again. I would ponder them. I would go to sleep thinking of the verses. After a week of unrest about the lost world, I said, "Oh, Father, I would love to go to the people who have never heard the gospel."

These verses were Romans 10:13-15:

> For whosoever shall call upon the name of the Lord shall be saved. How then shall they call on him in whom they have not believed? and how shall they believe in him of whom they have not heard? and how shall they hear without a preacher? And how shall they preach, except they be sent? as it is written, How beautiful are the feet of them that preach the gospel of peace, and bring glad tidings of good things!

I recalled the time after Jim and I were married. Our prayer became,

"Oh, Father, we are willing to go anyplace in this world. Just tell us where you want us to go."

This had been a long and difficult battle for Jim as he was going to be a "stateside preacher," not a missionary.

We started the process of appointment, since Jim was to be out of seminary in the fall. The question of where to go was answered when I heard a missionary say, "God often calls you to a place in which you are interested."

I hurried home and asked, "Jim, if you could go to any country in the world as a missionary, where would you go?" He answered without hesitation, "Colombia, South America."

Dr. and Mrs. Breeden were home on furlough and were living near the seminary. We found them eager to share with any young person interested in "their" Colombia. After many hours of seeing slides of the cities and hearing stirring stories from the lips of these great missionaries, our desire was linked to Colombia.

The procedure toward appointment is extremely long. As the days flowed into months, more and more excitement was generated about going to Colombia.

We filled out forms and wrote biographical sketches, doctrinal statements, and reference papers. Finally the physician was visited and the physicals completed. The Foreign Mission Board was also meeting today!

Our church was happy about their pastor's call. My GA girls had written a letter of congratulations, and our parents and friends were praying for us.

Jim dropped the receiver into its cradle. We both wept; we had been deferred. After three years of continued work in our church field, we could reapply if we were still interested.

My GA girls' speech of congratulations was silenced, and our friends didn't know what to say. Some of God's grand servants assured us we were needed at home, but our ears and hearts were open as never before.

We saw our church field. It was located between Fort Worth and Dallas (two towers of Southern Baptist life). Across the field from our church was another Southern Baptist church. A mile in any direction you would find another Southern Baptist church. The people of our area had heard the message of salvation time and time again.

We naturally turned our eyes to places where the gospel was rare. Our song leader revealed that in Ohio there were cities of 50,000 with no Baptist witness.

Jim took a job during the summer, earning enough money to make it possible for us to go and see this new world, a land of briars and Tennesseans without churches. Ohio was a bud about to flower in the Southern Baptist bouquet.

Jim was thrilled to be called as pastor of the Groesbeck Baptist Chapel, in a suburb of Cincinnati, Ohio. Groesbeck Baptist Chapel became our new challenge. It grew fast.

After the two and a half years we again said, "Father, we are still willing to go to Colombia, South America, as missionaries." The familiar forms had to be filled out. Our life sketches had to be updated. Again the day approached for the Board to decide.

Since Jim was away in a revival, I faced the ringing of the telephone by myself. The call came almost as soon as the Board had dismissed. It was a representative of the Board.

The voice on the other end of the line said, "Mrs. Bullis, the Foreign Mission Board met today. They spent much time in prayer and even longer in discussion. Your references were good, but we feel you both have avoided learning a foreign language. We think you would have difficulty with Spanish. We have unanimously decided you and Jim should not be appointed.

"We feel you would be happier in a large city of the United States where you could do the things you enjoy. Colombia is a Catholic country, and we are afraid you would become discouraged and would not stay long where you could not see great results.

"Please do not reapply since this is our final decision. We are sorry and appreciate your search for God's greatest will."

After saying good-bye, I sobbed, "But, God, we are willing!"

I dressed the five children and drove to the church where Jim was preaching. This one-hundred-mile trip seemed like a thousand.

After the services we wept and prayed, "Oh, Father, we are willing. Guide us to the mission field where you want us to serve. We want to seek your will." My desire had gone to the ends of the world, but my feet must be content to walk the path of Judea and Samaria.

A few weeks later we made a trip to the Ohio Baptist Convention office to meet with Dr. Ray Roberts and Dr. Arthur Walker. Jim asked them to suggest the most difficult field in the homeland. Dr. Walker suggested we look toward Buffalo, New York. This was an area where the gospel was barely beginning to penetrate.

O Father, may we see the fields which are ours with the same vision we have seen the uttermost parts of the world.

O Father, who chose Saul from among the baggage, help us to take seriously the task but not to take ourselves so seriously.

3
"Tryouts"

Jim's "trial sermons" during the past few years have been vastly different from those of most pastors. We haven't seen many pulpit committees, robed in their solemn cloaks of responsibility, enter hallowed church doors to ask Jim to "try out."

The first church which my husband pastored was a small Texas mission. This became ours only because we were in the right place at God's time. We joined this mission in our college town. After being a member only a short time, the pastor shared with us that he would graduate soon and resign from the mission. He added, "Jim, I think God wants you as the next mission pastor."

Hearing this, as a newlywed couple, we were sure he was mistaken. Both of us were green kids of nineteen. The mission had been started in the lower area of Brownwood to help the poor people who had many problems. The agreement of the mission committee of the mother church stirred us into searching for God's will. The mother church called Jim as pastor of the mission and ordained him.

Finishing college gave Jim the opportunity to turn the task of pastoring the mission over to another young man. We would have two months in school before moving to New Orleans to enter seminary. Jim's desire to preach during those months made him call the associational missionary and ask for the name of a church in need of a pastor.

A short drive into the country brought him face to face with a new breed. The deacon was a kind man. After Jim shared his desire to come and preach while still in school, the older deacon smiled, moving his "toback" to the other cheek. He looked into the sky past Jim, pushed his hands a little deeper into his overalls, and after a long minute of thought extended to Jim the opportunity to come. His invitation was, "Well, young man, I guess you can't hurt us any."

This little country church prior to our arrival had preaching monthly but now met every Sunday. After two months they asked us to consider going to seminary in Fort Worth instead of New Orleans. This we did. The drive was a two-hundred-and-thirty-mile round trip.

The calls to the next two churches were without incident, teaching us how it should be done.

Our move to pioneer missions marked the beginning of the strange calls or "tryouts" that can come only north of the Ohio River.

Jim had been enlisted to hold a revival after he had written and asked for the opportunity. We were to have a Vacation Bible School and a revival under a tent in a small, riverfront town across the Ohio River.

It was Thursday evening. The week was almost over. Just as the service was about to start, all eyes turned to the sound of a car coming down the road. The people who attended the revival were poorly dressed, and most were a little unkempt. They arrived on foot since they didn't have cars. The people who stepped from the car were well dressed. The three men were wearing suits and ties; the three women were well dressed in their hats, stockings, and heels. Their few comments as they entered the tent made it clear they did not want to say anything until they had "looked us over." I could see their expressions as the service was conducted. Even though they were trying to be careful not to show their feelings, I saw the smiles on their faces. I was not surprised when they asked to speak with us.

We stayed for the weekend, so we could attend their church. We found a small group of people meeting in a two-story house. It was as if we had known the people all our lives. The "tryout" was not difficult for the people were ready and willing to hear Jim. It seemed that God had planned us for each other.

After the evening service, we were told to step outside while they held a meeting. It was a beautiful mid-August evening. We stood together, waiting for their approval. They had certainly met our expectations. We were ready to race back to Texas, resign the church there, pack, and move in order to put our children into the Ohio school by September. The door opened. We were invited in as the pastor and wife of the Groesbeck Baptist Church, Cincinnati, Ohio.

Then came a call to the hardest field. The road was long between Cincinnati and Buffalo, New York. Some snow had fallen. In the suburbs of Buffalo, we found on that February day, piles of snow as high as the top of the street lights! We had been invited to "look over" the North Tonawanda Baptist Chapel.

We met one Southern Baptist family. A few people had Baptist backgrounds, but most were lacking much church experience. They had no training on how to "try out" preachers.

The building was old and beautiful. The windows could not merely be described with the word *magnificent*. They were radiant as their brilliant stained glass burst with color, fused together with molten lead.

We were met at the door by a few of the chapel's members. Our children were swept away to their classes, and Jim and I were ushered into the huge auditorium where a class of eight or nine adults was being taught by a young man from the mother church.

The teacher was a serious-faced young man with a lesson to present. Having the preacher who was "trying out" in his class would not bother him in the least. The introductions were brief, for the lesson was, of course, most important.

Pastor Jim gave this teacher his best attention. He listened to every word the solemn-faced teacher uttered. As time passed, Jim's mind drifted to the beauty of the building. He noticed the pews where we were sitting. The carving on the hymn book rack was a creation of art. On either side of the rack were three small holes for the Lord's Supper glasses. Jim slipped a finger into a hole. Then he slipped all three fingers into the holes, which were lined up together. Somehow the large third finger fit too tightly into the hole. He tried to remove it from the hole only to find that it stubbornly refused to yield. In fact, it was stuck tight.

Now, what does a preacher on his best behavior do in a situation like this?

His first interest was to get his finger out without disturbing those around him. He covered the immobile hand and pulled, while looking intently at the teacher. He hoped no one would notice his fingers which were blushing red from the pulling.

Minutes passed. Yet the finger, gaining affinity for its surroundings, was more firmly lodged than ever. This was serious; Jim realized he might have to preach his trial sermon while captured by the third-row pew! Jim decided he must give a very hard pull. He tugged as hard as he could, but his knuckle wedged in more tightly than ever.

The class member behind him noticed the preacher's movement and leaned up to see what was the problem. When his eyes fell on the red hand in the pew rack, his face broke into a grin. His eyes were riveted to the drama. The man next to him glanced over, and then away again. All of a sudden his eyes returned as if to say, *Did I see what I thought I saw?* A restrained laugh escaped his lips.

I looked over, horrified. How did Jim get himself into this fix? What would he do to escape? It was nearly time for the worship service. There was nothing I could do but watch the improbable spectacle before my eyes. When Jim wasn't pulling, he was covering his hand in hopes no one else would see his problem. He didn't want to further disturb the class. Others did see, and the laughter spread, forcing Jim to make a quick decision. If the teacher thought the class was laughing at him (the teacher), his feelings would be hurt. Jim knew he must confess.

He raised his free hand. The teacher, conducting the lesson as if nothing was happening, paused long enough to say, "Yes, would you like to add a thought?" "Oh, no! I just wanted to say the class is not laughing at you. It's laughing at me." As Jim said this he rose to show the teacher his dilemma. In the process of standing he added, "You see, I have my finger stuck in this hole." The standing made his finger straighten, and it slipped free. The laughter was unleashed. The solemn-faced teacher only cleared his throat and continued his lesson as if nothing had occurred.

After this "tryout" the chapel did call Jim as their pastor. He found they had a keen sense of humor and enjoyed a warm exchange of good-natured fun.

At the next "tryout" there would be no sermon, captive finger, or even a church building. There had been a Bible School in the Masonic temple. We enrolled 125 boys and girls. The next week Jim had a revival in the same temple. The revival was attended by over fifty children, plus Jim and a lady. How does a preacher reach out to a roomful of children? He tells them the best Bible stories they have ever heard.

Our desire to have a chapel on the eastern side of Buffalo led us to rent the building on Sunday mornings. I dropped off Jim and four of the children at the North Tonawanda Baptist Church, then Bob and I would drive twenty-two miles to Lancaster. We would go through the area and pick up children in our Volkswagen bus.

One day Mrs. Vi McDonald's car was being repaired. A friend had mentioned the strange woman and children who met for Sunday School in the Masonic temple. She decided to visit. As she and her daughter entered they felt needed.

Later our "tryout" took place at a restaurant table. Vi extended the call by saying, "Jim, we need a pastor here. North Tonawanda has sixty people. Why don't you and Mary move here and be our pastor?" We answered the call to represent Southern Baptists on the eastern side of Buffalo. It opened the door to another 300,000 people.

Our call was not merely for the area church, but to start missions. We had the privilege of extending calls to three mission pastors. They were: Brother Gilmore Samuelson, a native of Buffalo who came to pastor the Sullivan Road Chapel; Brother Curtis Monday, who arrived to shepherd the French Road Chapel; and Brother Ralph Fingerlow, a member of Veterans Park Baptist Church, who rented the YWCA building to attempt a work in Batavia, New York.

Our greatest "tryout" was before our Southern Baptist brethren. We moved across the border to the beautiful "Golden Horseshoe" area of Ontario, Canada, to start the first Southern Baptist chapel. If our "tryout" is successful, the Southern Baptist Convention will pick up on our dream. Our prayer is that our beloved Convention will respond to this challenge as it has to all others.

Dear Father, we know all events of life are but preparation for the greatest judgment. May its verdict be: "Well done, thou good and faithful servant."

4
Dilemma in
—————My First Pioneer—————
Mission Field

Our arrival in Cincinnati, Ohio, was foreknown and fashioned by the Holy Spirit. We knew the reason for our coming. God had called us. Our work would be to glorify him. But in six months the glory had faded and the fashioning was in shambles.

Changing from dillydallying in the Texas sun to tackling mountains of wet, frozen clothes was a shock. The short but repeated trips of the children into the frigid winter required a new kind of stamina.

Lack of space forced my husband into a church building program. Halloween had been the beginning of the building, while on Thanksgiving the men raised the trusses. December saw the roof shingles being laid. Christmas brought the dry wall going up, and in January and February the interior carpentry and painting were completed. There would be few hours Jim or the car would be home.

My family demanded I give up church worship since a trio of petty, capricious diseases teamed up against me. In this same November the home was invaded by measles. One after the other the children were sick. December ushered in the chicken pox. Those diseases chose to abide with us well into January.

On the first of January, my nine months came to an end. My last son was about to be born. The time came at five o'clock in the morning. I was thankful Jim was at home to take me to the hospital. He dropped me off at the hospital and carried the children to the home of one of our members. He hurried back to find Timothy had announced himself.

Jim glanced at his new, big, red-haired baby boy, checked to make sure we were both well, and said good-bye. He didn't return again until it was time to take me home from the hospital. The building of the church had to go on.

Some of the men had said, "Jim, take time to go see Mary."

"Oh, she understands," Jim said and kept on working.

I did understand, but the hospital rules made things hard for me. Only the father or mother could visit the maternity ward.

I called my mother in Missouri and said, "Mom, I know what an unwed mother must feel like. The only ones who can visit me are too far away or too busy." By evening my mother was on an airplane and soon was at my side.

The change in weather had created problems for David. At the slightest fever he would go into a convulsion. If he had a convulsion I felt I needed to be near, and as a result I never left him with a baby-sitter, or even a neighbor. I kept him near.

Putting all of these things together, I cried out, "Father, I see why Jim is here, but why am I here? What good can I do?"

God quietly spoke, but the truth evaded me.

Then came the awesome triumph of the mumps! I took the first child to the doctor's office. After looking at the lump below the earlobe he said, "Yes, he will have a good case of the mumps."

"Oh," I said, "I have pain in the neck just below the earlobe, too." You guessed it. I had the mumps, too.

This didn't seem to concern the doctor. He assured me that I would feel ill, but not to worry.

My next remark brought him to attention. "You know, I think Jim has them, too. He has a lump below his ear."

The doctor asked, "Where is he?"

"He has gone to get a load of tile for the church floor."

"Tell him to get home, not to unload the tile, and get to bed," ordered the doctor.

Jim surprised me when he obeyed the doctor's orders. By night I was very tired. I flopped into a chair and gave a yawn. My, it hurt. I thought it must be good to be a man and be ordered to bed with the mumps.

The Bullis family was absent from church the next Sunday, all sharing a common adventure with the mumps in various stages. David, the sick child, never fell to the mumps invasion.

The building, which was previously started, was ready for services the first Sunday of February. I was able to attend! It was a thrill to see over one hundred people in church that Sunday.

There were many tears that first service, some due to the thrill of having the new building almost completed, and others because the furnace did not work. Large blowers had been lit to keep the people warm. The blowers created fumes in the room, causing tears. All the people cried for joy, or of necessity.

With these currents and eddies around me, my ship was going nowhere.

I prayed, "O Father, why am I here?"

The Father seemed to say, "Mary, look and see what you can use to serve me."

I realized I had very little with which to serve him. I had always tried to be the best pastor's wife I could be. But now . . .

My only contact with the world seemed to be my telephone. I took it in hand. Next I saw a stack of old, dusty survey cards left from the hard work of the summer missionaries the year before we came. In the process of building they were neglected. As I called the number on the first card, I prayed and asked God to help me use my time to further his kingdom.

The stack of cards came alive. They were no longer dusty cards, but names and addresses of friends whom I could invite to church—I could share the message of Christ with them. The first Sunday, one of the people whom I had called came to church. My heart was full of joy.

I called a friend, Lou, a young mother who had the same problem, and shared some of my cards. She joined my ministry.

My lesson from the Lord during these trying months was, "Mary, what do you have in your hand? Use it for me. Use it, and I will give direction to your ship on the sea of life. Even though the storms rage about you, when I am ready, I will calm the storms and still the winds of your life."

O Lord, may I never forget to search for your will during the times when life seems empty, full, or even diverted. For when I find your kingdom's work, all other things are added.

O Father, who used the loaves and fishes, what tools can we use to teach the children today?

5
My
—————— Boastful ——————
Friend

I have asked my friend to write the next story and will edit it to prevent him from becoming too boastful.

I arrived at the Groesbeck Baptist Church's parsonage in the spring of 1964 in a large shipping box. Pastor Bullis signed for my delivery and then hurriedly carried me into the house. He carelessly yanked my box open and jerked me into the living-room floor, unveiling my ungainly, ugly bulk.

Pastor Bullis's large hands grabbed my handle and opened my large, silver mouth. Power flowed as the plug was connected. My motor whirled, causing my sharp teeth to revolve in my large, silver mouth.

The smile of delight on the pastor's face showed he was pleased. The packing slip read $69.00. A look around the room revealed five small children and old furniture. Someone wanted me pretty badly to spend a week's salary for me. The money could have been used for other things.

In the next few days I was proudly introduced. My gifts were shared with several small Bible Schools.

The pastor's words of praise for my work at the pastors' conference were much too tame. For I was the first one of my kind to be used in Vacation Bible Schools in Ohio's Southern Baptist churches. My ability to draw children and create enthusiasm would bring others of my kind.

By our second summer together, I was to draw children to the largest Bible School in the association. The pastor ordered a large circus tent. The furniture was moved from the living room of the parsonage. Even my competition was ousted from the parsonage garage. The job of moving the furniture from the living room was soon accomplished, but the garage was something else.

Pastor Bullis was a "junk collector," but he called it usable material. Can you imagine fifteen large teachers' desks stacked three high in the garage? These were embedded in three dump-truck loads of children's chairs. I forced them to be used or given away. My coming changed things!

The chairs were needed in the Bible School. They were placed in the living room, in the large circus tent, every corner of the church, and even spread out to the neighborhood members' garages. Really, they demanded a lot from me! I ground my teeth incessantly, since so much depended upon my help to make this the largest Bible School in the association and, possibly, in the state. It was a great week. We enrolled over four hundred boys and girls.

I was rewarded by . . . being stuck back into my box in the garage with those silly chairs! I who had been the star of every leaflet which sang my praises.

Later, boxes were stacked all about the garage, and a rental truck was pulled up to the parsonage. The truck was loaded with fifty chairs and furniture. Would they leave *me* behind? No, I was placed on top of two desks. I sat enthroned like a king!

The truck rolled north through Ohio, turned east through Pennsylvania, and entered the state of New York. When the doors were flung open at an old house in North Tonawanda, New York, I felt the same feeling as when I worked—COLD! Everywhere I looked, I saw ice. My, it must have taken some machine to make so much ice!

Pastor Bullis began to make plans for my summer job. This would be a great adventure. It was rumored I would fail. Even my abilities would not bring children to Bible School in Western New York.

When the time of truth came, I was faced with a dangerous rival. Pastor Bullis had always been pleased with my product; yet, he borrowed another machine. This machine didn't grind ice into a white, snow-like substance shaped by a cone paper cup flavored with syrup. Instead the inferior machine scorched sugar with an imitation flavor around a cardboard cone into a hairy, cotton mess. They called it "Cotton Candy," but I called it "Hot 'n Tacky!" It certainly wasn't cool like me.

After a big parade through the streets, the children were led back to the churchyard to ride on a small circus train and have cotton candy and, of course, my delicious "Sno Cones," which were not tacky. I broke all records, with just a little help.

Before I arrived in the Western New York area, the Frontier Baptist Association had enrolled only about 500 in Bible Schools. My appearance picked things up. The association enrolled over 1,100! The next summer over 1,700 enrolled and the next, over 2,200. I had introduced "Sno Cone Evangelism."

The associational director of missions, Brother Charles Magruder, bought a Sno Cone machine. The pastor of our mother church, Brother Curtis Porter, purchased a bright shiny machine. The number of Sno Cone machines grew from my small beginning to a tribe of seven machines.

During the summer of 1978, Pastor Bullis, Mrs. Bullis, Virginia Bullis, along with Mrs. Lois Dunnaway of Durnin, South Carolina, and Lois Harbridge drove twenty-two miles to the eastern side of Buffalo. We went to have a Bible School in the park. My job was to ensure success.

When we arrived at Como Park in Lancaster, I failed. They were able to find only two children. They blamed it on some destructive rumors.

Pastor Bullis had to call upon my talents. He placed me in back of the station wagon and drove to a needy section. He saw a group of children playing. He stopped the car. "Would you like a Sno Cone? Go get your mother, and I will give you a Sno Cone," he said.

The children scurried in all directions. When they returned with a few mothers to check this stranger out, Pastor Bullis told them who I was and why he wanted the children to come to Bible School in Como Park. He let me work with electric power provided from an outside plug of one of the children's homes. After the mothers and children had tasted my delicious product and had a chance to get to know Pastor Bullis, a crowd came to Bible School. I succeeded in spite of rumors and the workers' fears.

Pastor Bullis saw another group of children near a building. It was a tavern. His desire to give the children Sno Cones made him enter the tavern and get permission to use the outside electrical plug. I didn't like this idea at all, so I choked on my ice, blowing the first, second, and a third fuse. I had never worked on tavern power before or since. I closed that tavern down for a short time!

Two years later the Bullis family moved me to the eastern side of Buffalo. Where would we start in that area? Pastor Bullis began with me. Into parks, playgrounds, and backyards we went. One summer I provided my sweet-flavored product to 1,476 boys and girls enrolled in eighteen parks.

After serving faithfully for sixteen years, fourteen of them with Pastor Bullis and two with the pastor at Alden, I was not allowed to go on the next mission venture. My strong legs were getting weak, and my teeth had been replaced several times. I suffered from the fear of my motor losing its power, so they put me into semiretirement.

A brand-new machine was given by a friend as we entered Canada. If he works as hard as I did, there will be many children flocking to hear about Jesus.

The new machine will have the honor of working from Niagara Falls to Toronto. From Lake Ontario west to Kitchener and London.

In my own way I have become a cup of cold water given in the name of Christ to the least of mankind.

Old but happy,

The Sno Cone Machine

Lord of the little ones, I thank you for the joy of discovering small things with which to accomplish large dreams. May the ones who have tasted blue raspberry Sno Cones remember your loving grace.

6
My
——————Father's——————
Eyes

I have said many times, "A person who has never seen a miracle never has needed one." Oftentimes we preplan, preprogram, and prepurchase proposed accomplishments. Our strengths become our weaknesses. We leave little room for God's working.

It is different in pioneer missions. The lack of resources brings utter dependence upon the Father.

The Father must have been watching as we moved to the church in Cincinnati, Ohio. It was meeting in a two-story house where the living/dining room served as an auditorium. The children sat at Jim's feet, playing with his shoe laces.

Due to Jim's promise to begin a building, the two-year-old plans from the architectural commission were brought to the building committee. Nothing had been done because of the appraised price of the building which was many times more than the church could borrow.

The Father must have looked down and must have seen the need, for he sent a man who was a builder of attractive homes. Jim told the builder of his dilemma. This Christian man called his trained cost analyst to break the building down into minor subcontracts, material lists, labor costs, and so forth.

In a few days Jim had the estimated lowest cost for each construction stage, along with performance contracts to be signed by subcontractors. Jim became a building contractor.

The next hurdle was the complicated county building laws. The county inspector penciled in red: footing depths, needed roof pitches, additional doors, and the like. When finished he stamped the plans and filed them. He must have had compassion on the preacher who knew so little about building. The building was erected for one third of the estimated cost.

The church had an option to buy the land including a house within the year. Although this doubled the church loan, the Father gave them the faith to mortgage the present for the future. Later, the front property sold for seven times its original cost.

My Father had so much to care for as we prepared to move to Western New York. We had been on half salary the past year, and just before we moved the car slung a rod, meaning a new motor was necessary. After the hard move, we found it would be six weeks before our first paycheck. Having never worked at an office job, I was amazed when I was hired for a part-time job. God had provided our daily bread.

I am sure the Father's eyes had been on the house we moved into during the one hundred years it had stood. It took one fourth of our salary to support its utility habits. Jim said, "We can't afford an old house, but we could build a new one if we had a piece of land."

I found a lady who was selling part of her yard. Her price was hundreds of dollars below similar lots. The bank agreed to give the church a loan for the land and materials if we would do the labor ourselves. The church's pastors would then enjoy low-housing costs.

The Father had heard the ringing of the old church bells since 1876. The cost of maintaining the ancient building made it necessary to start a day-care center. We knew the Father would delight in the little ones sharing his building.

We were convinced that prayer and Bible stories should be the center of our program. We were told that this was not possible. The regional director from Rochester, New York, was called in. It was her job to make the decision on our license. This lovely woman, in a high position, shared that she was God's friend. She then suggested we should make changes in the proposed request. These would clearly state that our church would accept no public funds, including surplus commodities.

How happy the Father must have been to hear the little children's laughter and praise.

We had accepted the challenge of outreach on the eastern side of Buffalo. A couple from Tennessee visited the homes of the children enrolled in our two park Bible Schools in the Depew-Lancaster area. Their goal was to have a Bible study in the park at the end of the week.

The loving Father must have smiled knowingly on Friday when the sun went down on their dreams. Not one person attended. He hurt for them as they spiritually limped into our house. With haggard faces they commented, "We tried, but we honestly feel no work will begin soon in the eastern side of the city."

He knew our new Sunday School would begin before the close of the year. It was born in the Masonic temple and would grow into the Veterans Park Baptist Church and its chapels.

Just before Thanksgiving, 1969, we moved to the eastern side of Buffalo to start the first Southern Baptist church. At this time there was no church pastoral supplementary aid available for any new work. Jim had planned to go to the Buffalo School Board to apply for a substitute teaching position. To his surprise they reluctantly accepted his application. He was warned that he would never be called to teach. They had five-hundred certified substitutes, and half of these received less than two or three days per year. Jim was not certified.

It must have been the Father who directed the call for Jim's service the next week. It couldn't have been man's choice. The classes extended for the rest of the week. He was quickly placed on the top of the list, receiving all the days he would accept.

During this time I was opening a "Pandora's Box." Depew, the church's location, was more than 90 percent Catholic, while the town board was 100 percent. They were horrified at the application for an occupancy permit for the use of our church building as a day-care center. They felt a Baptist church was not a place for child care. For five months we attended town board meetings, met all physical demands, and presented the needs for a center in the twin cities. There wasn't one at that time.

The Father must have helped the town mayor and the town's electrician to see the unfairness, and they helped to bring about a new day for community services by the churches. During our ten years in the area, the town board became responsive to our many requests.

The church-building loan was granted to a very small group of members solely on the strength of the day-care center.

As an outgrowth of the Bible Schools, our church voted to buy a bus. Ten families gave nine-hundred dollars. This amount was one-half the asking price from the commercial firms.

The Father must have directed Jim to a department of transportation official. The kindly man said, "I cannot give information of private companies who have buses for sale, but have you ever seen the small town of Newfane? It's a delightful, weekday trip. By the way, there is a Catholic school-bus garage which could give you many ideas on the upkeep of buses. Why don't you take a drive out to Newfane?"

The trip proved profitable. The price of the bus was nine-hundred dollars. They had two of them for sale. As far as we know, this began the earliest bus ministry by Southern Baptists in New York State.

The Father saw the small church in Depew working the eastern side of Buffalo. The size of the program left few pennies in the pot for a pastor's salary. Church camps, bus ministries, park Bible Schools, and church expenses became our greatest personal adversary. Their demands had to be met if the church were to continue. It would take thousands of dollars every year.

Jim came home from teaching school one day and said, "Mary, what would you say if I spent $300 to $400 this month?" That was a full month's salary.

I asked him, "What for?" He then shared a feeling that the New York State buses could meet a need of Southern Baptist churches. He wanted to locate buses for sale that churches desiring buses could purchase. The telephone would be his direct line to both. From New York City to Jamestown, Watertown to the Pennsylvania border, he sought bus-bid lists of school systems. He made calls from Florida to Louisiana, Virginia to Mississippi to find his first customers. It took three months to sell the first bus. This became the second-largest source of church income during the next four years.

The angels were watching and rejoicing as 300 children were enrolled in the French Road Park Bible School in Cheektowaga, New York. This was New York's fastest-growing area at that time. The center of the community was three acres of land on the main street, French Road. The land held a beautiful old house and three antiquated barns which were eyesores.

The Father's eyes looked toward the future, and certainly there must have been a twinkle as we knocked on the door of the house. Jim said to the elderly lady who answered, "We would like to rent part of your house for church services."

We listened very closely to her frightened speech, "NO! NO! Me live here. Me cats and dogs live here. Me Cad-o-lic."

The Father had foreseen the "For Sale" sign placed in the yard three years later. He knew the asking price of the property was $87,000, to be divided equally among three different sets of heirs. He was present at our business meeting called to discuss the property. A big, lovable auctioneer said, "Offer $52,000 and no more."

"Why?" Jim asked.

The auctioneer answered, "The Father can give it to us for a smaller amount as easily as a larger one if he wants us to have it."

The real-estate dealer laughed and didn't take the offer to the sellers. Two more years had to pass. Just three days after the New York 1977 blizzard, Jim and I went out to see the piles of snow.

Coming to the French Road property, we couldn't see the "For Sale" sign, for it was snow-covered. Jim went to the back door and knocked. A young lady listened as he said, "We are still willing to pay $52,000 for this property for a church."

She stopped him, "A church? You said a church? Give me your telephone number. I will get back to you."

The heirs had a meeting in which they discussed their mother's oft-repeated words, "Me bad. . . . Should have let my house be church."

The Father must have said, "Now is the right time." So French Road Chapel found its home.

As the writer of Hebrews said, "And what shall I more say? for the time would fail me to tell of . . . " (Heb. 11:32). Worthless land made valuable, water from dry wells, gas well on property, banks going against their practices, churches moving from auditoriums and educational space so we might have a home and meeting place.

No time to tell of hospital bills paid by miracles, cars dead yet running, brakes failing on buses while stopped, bottomless barrels of dented cans of food surfacing when needed most, houses and barns burning, yet the pastor's family brought forth.

Nor can I write much about the estimated 7,000 New Testaments freely given, or of the hundreds of people who "have obtained a good report" through finding faith in trusting Jesus Christ.

O Father, thank you for giving me the substance of things hoped for and the evidence of things not seen.

Lord, maker of the mountains, can you help me to see all tasks in proportion to your strength?

7
Mountains
—to—
Possess

Caleb seemed to have one foot in the grave, yet he went looking for the hardest mountain and conquered it. From its peak, he watched as his enemies retreated past the younger men below.

My desire is to have the stamina of Caleb.

Instead, I have a tendency to say to the mountain, "Be cast into the sea," "Get out of my path," or "Let someone else enter the mountain besides me."

I look at the plow. The hardest part of any plowing is taking hold of the handles. Plowing is difficult, and the toil is drudgery. Why not let others handle the plow? The task of getting started is often more difficult than the labor of the whole job.

I stood in my kitchen relieving the evening dishes of their burden of rejected foods. A family of seven leaves a sizable mound of soiled Melmac and utensils. I thought pleasantly, *how nice it would be to have a dish washer.*

The pastors' meeting had been unusually long. I knew my husband in his role as the new pastor would try to instill a few of his past theories.

The dishes were done. The children had gone to bed when Jim walked in. I tried to seek out, by my overly attentive attitude, what had taken place at the pastors' meeting. Jim was withdrawn and quiet. He refused to note my "relaxed-but-searching" spirit. "I'm tired. It was a long meeting," he said as he went down the stairs. "I'll be right down after I turn off the lights," I said after him. He turned away without a word. Disturbed as I was, I didn't realize my good fortune.

Jim finally said, "Mary, I suggested a youth camp for the association." I exclaimed, "How wonderful!" "They wanted to hire a cook or have the food brought in." His next remarks were repeated in a whisper. "I knew we couldn't afford such a camp." I replied, "Yes, if the camp's price is too high, our youth couldn't afford to attend." Jim then repeated what Pastor Porter had said, "Mary and Jim have seven in their family; they cook for more people than anyone else. Why not turn the cooking over to them?"

I sat up straight in bed. "Jim! You didn't, did you?" I didn't want to take on that mountain. "It makes sense; besides I'll do the buying and the ordering," Jim persuaded me quickly. The mountain was there. I was to cook and bake for seventy-five to one hundred people.

The ordering took two months. We had to discover how much milk, bread, and other food the campers would eat. The supplies were to be transported in our Volkswagen bus.

Never had a Volkswagen been called upon for a more heroic task! Cases and cases of food were needed. One hundred loaves of day-old bread and three, five-gallon containers of milk were included. We had a veritable mountain of fresh vegetables, fruits, and cases of eggs—all this from following the guidelines of nutrition to the letter.

The bus, sitting on its springs, groaned to the state thoroughfare. The collector at the tollgate looked at the heads of the children poking out from the space on top of the boxes. They were forced to lie in the small space between the boxes.

"You almost have a load," was the toll collector's friendly greeting.

The Volkswagen had a moment's pause, as the determined "pops" of the small motor complained under its load. We still had one more stop for supplies.

The frozen meat was to be placed near the front door. It had to be taken from the bus first. Near the door meant on the seat at my right side, only inches from my body.

As the week progressed, the hamburger became spaghetti and Salisbury steaks. I have never seen such a huge pile of white-and-red "yarn" waiting to be consumed. There were over three hundred meatballs, all seasoned just right. It was enough to make an Italian's palate cry, "Surrender."

The Salisbury steaks were lovingly formed, patted, and baked. When the first camper looked at the nicely browned Salisbury steaks, he screamed in a melodramatic voice, "GAINSBURGERS!" Laughter spread throughout the good-humored campers. The hoots and hollers brought tears to my eyes. Camper after camper passed by the "Gainsburgers." Less than half of the Salisbury steaks were eaten. We had a run on the peanut butter and jelly.

The most interesting moment of the cooking came during the roast-beef dinner. Jim was called away from camp. Before leaving he said, "Mary, make the gravy. Follow the directions on the side of the commercial gravy jar."

I read:

> Place five gallons of water in a large pot and bring to a boil. Add two pounds of margarine and the contents of this jar in the boiling water. Make a paste by adding a box of cornstarch to water. Pour into the large pot and boil until the liquid thickens.

I followed the directions carefully. Soon the liquid turned into a hearty, brown gravy. In fact, gallons and gallons of hearty, brown gravy.

When Jim returned to camp he viewed it with a deep concentration. He said, "You made five gallons of gravy for seventy-five people? That is a gallon for every fifteen campers."

Needless to say, we catered our epicurean broth to the willing campers. The bowls on the tables were refilled as soon as they were emptied. Alas, we had three gallons left. We served gravy with every meal. It was a veritable widow's barrel. It never emptied. The camp director offered frozen gravy popsicles, but he had no takers! The funeral of the gravy came, after Jim said in a very firm voice, "The gravy popsicles must be eaten. The loser of the softball game will consume the last of them." The counselors were pitted against the campers. My friends, the counselors, were sure to lose. Wanting to prevent this "reward" to the volunteers who had worked so faithfully, I took the gravy to the sink and with some words of eulogy let it go. All three gallons disappeared down the drain.

Later, the green-faced counselors returned to the kitchen, defeated. I was thankful that they would find leftover cake, pudding, and pie.

The great gravy feast had passed into oblivion. I stood as Caleb, at the peak of my mountain, and watched as one of my enemies, "fear," fled away. The next summer there would be more campers, and every summer after that there would be mountains to possess.

After standing on the peak like Caleb, my molehill of Melmac and utensils seemed very small.

Thank you, Father, that the same hollow of your hand which holds the mountains will bear me up as I labor to reach the peak.

8
──────Vacation Plus──────

The summer program was at an end. But what an end! We had enrolled 1,475 boys and girls in eighteen park Bible Schools on the eastern side of Buffalo. We had 450 children enrolled in day camp or day care.

I had driven the church bus, worked with various programs, and had been responsible for supplying the workers with their various needs. I was errand girl, cook, and mother. There had been seventeen or more at our table for every meal. These seventeen included my four sons, one daughter, Christian Service Corps workers, six college-age workers, plus my husband and myself. At some of the meals we numbered as many as seventy, and for one solid week there were twenty-one in "our family."

This was more than enough for an association, let alone one small church with under forty in attendance. My actual job was pastor's wife and mother. It was a task I dearly loved, but it was one that had made me very tired.

Jim said, "Mary, you need a vacation." Jim wanted to take the two younger boys and me away for the last week of August.

Since we had been in New York, we had never really had a vacation, and that was an impossible idea for my mind to grasp. I found myself thinking of the places we could go: the Smoky Mountains, the city of New York, the long-desired trip to Washington, or a visit to my home. This was too good to be true. I would sleep late every day; I would have no dishes to do; I would have the opportunity to set a lazy pace. It would be grand! My tired mind rejoiced at the visions of rest.

I wondered what Jim was thinking of for money. I asked him where he was taking us. He said, "Camp Iron Bell for a few days."

That was a two-hour trip for us. It had a large 96-by-96-feet log cabin built in the shape of a cross. It had a tower room 32 feet by 32 feet. It also had an unfinished roof that needed to be shingled. It didn't take me long to realize who would be the roofing crew—my husband Jim, Tim, David, and I. I smiled and said, "At least there won't be any dishes."

Now this didn't normally come under the task of a pioneer pastor's wife's job. Yet, in the past I had helped to roof the auditorium of a church and a parsonage our family built, plus the house we were living in. I had laid many a shingle but nothing this large. It would be like roofing five houses.

The boys were eager, and we drove down after church and slept in two cabins. I liked that part of the vacation. The sounds were restful and the weather delightfully cool. The morning came as early as any I had spent during the summer. It had rained during the night, and we walked out to a clear day.

The roof was like a sliding board, and the shingles kept sliding off the roof. We had to start on the job, standing at the edge looking down. I gave good advice until the shingles were at least five rows up. Then I joined the crowd of clacking hammers and swishing shingles sliding into place. I was almost as fast as they were, and besides, my rows were neater. We finished one whole roof on the first day, with the boys working their hardest.

I was so sore after the day's work that I felt I couldn't move my arms, and that I would walk with a permanent bend in my back. My shoulders felt as if there were a load that needed to be lifted. I was *sore*.

In the cabin in the small teen-size beds, a mattress covering plywood, I knew I was going to have to have some comfort. I got ready for bed by flashlight and asked Jim to rub the Ben Gay into my sore arms and back. He did it with more laughter than sympathy. I really couldn't sleep because I stung all over.

The next morning I heard the peck-peck of the hammers on the roof. I knew that there was a good reason for a farmer's wife to want to chop the head off the old, red-combed rooster. In any case, I wanted to get at that red-haired husband. What a terrible time to start—6:30 in the morning. He and Byron Lutz, the camp owner and director, felt they had to finish the task in a day. I went to join them, and the dew made the roof like a greased pig's back. I climbed up and worked a little slower.

The boys were still going like a house on fire. They would finally slow down on this second day.

David sat down on a shingle and with a yell went sliding off the roof. I saw him go over the side of the roof. I listened for the crash. He stuck his head up before I could get to him, both of us laughing. He had enjoyed that. I walked very carefully for a while.

That second night was the worst of all. I knew the Lord was going to take me home. No one could feel as bad as I did and still be alive. I decided I would rub my own back. I slipped out of the bed, without finding the flashlight, and felt until I found the Ben Gay tube. I took off the cap and rubbed the soothing salve on my back and arms.

My husband and Byron were on the roof as I opened my eyes. I got up to get dressed. As I picked up the brush beside the personal items, I saw the two tubes laying side by side. There was the small, nearly empty tube of Ben Gay and the large, fat tube of Pepsodent toothpaste.

I laughed, looking at my white arms. I had rubbed my arms and back with toothpaste. As I walked to the lodge I was still laughing. I picked up my hammer and nails and shared the best medicine with Jim and Byron. I had to listen as Pastor Byron Lutz began to sing at the top of his voice: "I wonder where the pain went . . . As you rub with Pepsodent."

Jim said as we came down from the roof, "Happy anniversary, Mary." It had been a wonderful way to spend our twenty-third anniversary.

By the end of the last day we had finished most of the four roofs. It was weathered in. Brother Lutz's dream was a little nearer completion, and we had a part in it. We had discovered that even this difficult task had become an enjoyable vacation. There were no tourist attractions. We didn't drive many miles. I didn't sleep late. We didn't spend any money, but. . . .

We had no expensive dinner on our twenty-third anniversary, but we had bread that men knew not of. There had been a feeling that a task was worth the effort. It had been a blessing to give our time as summer missionaries and others had freely given to us during the summer.

Thank you, Father, for making the hard tasks enjoyable, when it is done for you in the company of friends and family.

9
A Tribute to
—————Pioneer Pastors'—————
Children

A chapter must be dedicated to the children of pioneer pastors. They often serve as the unpaid and forgotten missionaries. Youthfully they replace the adults in many tasks. On our mission fields they shovel snow at our houses, proceed to the church driveway to free the frozen-in church buses, and finally attack 500 feet of church sidewalk, plus breaking the stubborn ice from the front steps. This changed with the coming of summer when they cut the grass in our yards, the church yards, and the grass at the house next door. Sometimes we expected them to help mow seven acres of grass at the camp site or cut and remove hawthorn trees, or scrape and paint buildings, or sand buses preparatory to painting them.

But the most-fussed-about job came repeatedly with the approach of each new summer program. Every Sunday afternoon when others were playing ball, our family, plus missionaries and a few others, were passing out in new communities hundreds of advertising leaflets to promote the upcoming Vacation Bible School. The kids have been chased and bitten by dogs, mocked by school chums, have had holes worn in their shoes, and have had to endure the curses of adults.

One day when Bob was very young, he was left behind to do a short street. When Jim returned he discovered Bob on the ground, covering his leaflets. The two mocking bullies who stood over him fled as they saw Jim approaching. As Jim picked up Bob, the little one said: "I didn't let them do it. They were going to throw my papers down the gutter."

After many years of this tiring job, week after week all summer long, they grew weary and probably would have been willing for any large or small bully to take their Bible School "slingers" and throw them away.

Yet, the most degrading task came once a year, usually in the spring. So I have asked the culprits to report the "true" account.

"High in our home, the bell tower of the church, you would find our congregation perched in uneven rows. Our gathering of church pigeons was more frequent than the gathering of the Baptists below. Our flapping wings couldn't be said to resemble the cherubims' wings. And our coos weren't those of the heavenly dove, but our family had fifty years of previous seniority. Those Baptists were the newcomers.

"We pigeons came to expect the Bullis boys to clean our five-foot-square breeding-bath-toilet-bedroom each year.

"When they purchased the old church building, no one had even noticed us, but as the snows came our "penthouse" crowd doubled, for our small bodies found the warm currents escaping through the floor and ceiling of the tower most soothing.

"When the snow melted, it was mixed with our debris running down the walls of the vestibule, demanding our spring cleaning. At one point during a hushed time of silent prayer a lady's voice cut through the silence, 'Whew, it smells like a chicken coop!' Time to house clean!

"The next Saturday the pastor got the task underway. He entered, as usual, our filthy tower with a bucket in hand and followed by a gagging son. They filled and lowered it to the equally upset boys below. As the dangling buckets descended, some of their contents would shower the boys. The boys emptied the refuse into garbage cans that were later unloaded into the flower beds. The boys repeated this until the tower was empty. We returned to our God-given roost which was now as clean as our servants could make it.

"Now, after several years of this, the neatest of the preacher's sons became very hostile and sought a way to discharge his feelings. He gathered a pocketful of stones, marched directly below our lofty station, and glared.

"We sat all in a row cooing, alternately serenading him and reminding him, 'You will never get rid of us!'

"He flung a missile at us. The sound of its fury warned us and we took to the air. When we returned to the tower, we raised our distressed coos, scolding him for disturbing our enjoyment of our newly cleaned domicile. He unleashed another projectile and again we retreated into the air, returning to scold him. This small battle was repeated many times with no harm done to us.

"Becoming weary of the boy, we called a pigeon business meeting. We decided to vent our anger on this red-haired pest who had brought great persecution upon us. A motion was made by our most demanding mother pigeon that the head deacon pigeon should go down and right the situation.

"The motion was seconded, and we fluttered our wings to show we were in favor. There was a call for objections, and, of course, there were none.

"Deacon pigeon flew from the tower to administer the discipline. Swooping down as the young man turned to go home, deacon pigeon let go, then flew away cooing as if to say, 'That should teach you a lesson.' The boy was disgusted, for his red hair and once-clean shirt were splashed with the well-aimed missile. The boy ran into the house angry and embarrassed."

Later the bell tower was sealed and the pigeons became homeless.

Father, I thank you for our children who have worked by our side to do so many unpleasant jobs. They were not perfect in attitude or even in completion, but much was accomplished, for they became extensions of our lives, ministry, and dreams. They carried loads too heavy and too demanding over long years. May you bless all pioneer pastors' children who labor beside their parents in strange cities, villages, small towns, in areas where "the fields are white unto harvest" and the mature reapers are so few.

O Father, you said the little ones could come to you, can you provide shelter, as does a mother hen, for my children since we cannot be there?

10
Giants
—in—
Our Land

Grabbing the only weapon she could find, her shoe, she darted out the door.

The bully was too busy doing his mischief. He didn't notice this little wisp of a girl coming down the walk. If he had noticed, he would have laughed the laughter of Goliath as young David approached.

Even though Virginia was a year and a half older than Daryl, her small frame was dwarfed by the "husky" size of her brothers.

In most neighborhoods you find the neighborhood bully. The victim of the bully is a year or two younger and a head shorter. Ours was no exception. The bully was Virginia's age and flaunted his size.

The bully attacked at the front of our house, forcing Daryl to the ground. Brother Bob, still younger, jumped in with a feverish frenzy. The two brothers were no match for their opponent.

With shoe in hand, Virginia, flung herself into action. The shoe hammered across his arm; it drilled across his back; it planed across his face. The shock of the blows was devastating. This small girl's confidence made him turn and run.

The boys refused to broadcast their shame, and Virginia was always protective of her brothers; consequently the story was not repeated.

Later I heard the bully say as he passed the house, "Watch out for the little, red-headed girl. She chased me down the street with her shoe."

Yes, I thought. *She is little but mighty.*

This sliver of a girl would find many giants in her path. It would take a variety of shoes to conquer them.

Virginia was fourteen years old when we moved to the eastern side of

Buffalo. It brought her new problems during a crucial time of her life. She was shy and found that 95 percent of the pupils in her high school were Roman Catholics. The majority tended to exclude those of different religious backgrounds.

An ugly and frightening monster was loneliness. To deal with it, she escaped into her world of books and studies. Her reading and study habits kept her ahead of the students in her classes. Praise flowed her way as she brought home As on her report cards. Her teachers' words of praise were muted with "but she is so shy."

On graduation day, Virginia won a battle over her giant. This victory would give her confidence to win many other struggles. Out of 245 graduates, she was not the most noticeable.

The band began, words of welcome were extended, and the special moment had come. Virginia was introduced and invited to the rostrum. She, the lonesome duckling, stepped forward to be praised as a swan. The speech, lovingly nurtured at home, was presented with strained voice and rigid spine. It was the usual greeting, but she went on to admonish her classmates to seek God's strength. The message was one she lived.

The speech was listed as the "Salutatory Oration." Virginia had made the second-highest grade in this large class. My eyes filled with tears, realizing the giant had lost, and Virginia had secured a genuine victory. She finished her speech, smiled, and returned to her chair.

The summer vacation passed quickly. We were now taking Virginia to the airport. Without a tear, our little girl kissed us good-bye and made her way down the ramp. In a few hours she would be at college, 650 miles away from home.

In the quiet of the car, I flung myself into Jim's arms and wept. Through my sobs, I cried, "Oh, Father, I will miss her so. She is so small and inexperienced. There are so many Goliaths out there.

"Father, I pray that your ever-surrounding love and our unending love will reach across the miles to be missiles with which she can fight her giants.

"I have had her for such a short time. Now she will be away from the shelter of our wings and must depend upon your protection and strength."

As we rode home in silence, I thought about how quickly the time would come for Daryl, Bob, Dave, and Tim to leave our shelter.

O Father, you have so much love. I pray you will help me love each of my boys every day with your kind of love. Amen.

O Father, who helped young David slay his lion, can you give youth the roots of victory for tomorrow?

11
The
—————— Leader of ——————
Many

God, in his wisdom, gave each of our children different personalities with which to meet their problems.

Daryl would face the same Catholic community as his sister, but would find his own way to handle his encounters. His twin spirit would be his strength. One of these was named "love," the other "determination." With these two he would disarm those around him. His name was not on the dean's list. He would never be invited to the Honor Society, but he received his honors.

One day while driving down the street, I saw a large boy force Daryl from the sidewalk. I stopped the car and Daryl got in.

I asked, "Daryl, why did you step from the sidewalk to let that boy pass?"

"Ma (that's 'Mother' in New York), I had no choice. He's bigger but someday he'll move for me."

This may have been one of the reasons why Daryl joined the wrestling team. The first year his team was a loser. They wrestled seventeen matches and lost sixteen.

I shall never forget seeing my first wrestling match. Oh, I hurt every time Daryl was flung to the floor! I closed my eyes as he endured the crucifix, cross-body ride, and arm lock. I breathed a sigh of relief when the referee blew the whistle.

At home I said, "Daryl, why are you doing this? Why do you put yourself through so much only to lose and see your team lose?"

"Ma, next year will be different."

Next year *was* different. Daryl not only wrestled, but he brought his brothers into the arena. Bob was wrestling at his side, and Dave was a manager. Even Tim was being groomed in the middle of our living-room floor for later years.

That year Jim and I became involved. I cleared my calendar to make room for the matches. Our presence became very important, not only to our boys but to their coaches.

The third year was exciting. The losing team had become a winning one. The community was shocked by their record. I eagerly grabbed the newspaper to see the sports page. I would laugh as I read, "Bullis Brothers Shine" or "Brothers Win Again."

Winning didn't just happen. The Bullis boys spent many hours in practice. They were so disciplined to the task of winning that my menus were determined by their sport.

Daryl was cocaptain during the third year. His spirit of love was very evident. He became like a mother hen to the other wrestlers. I would watch him during the matches. As each wrestler performed, he would be nearby pacing the floor giving them encouragement. He would call words of praise and instructions to them. Often, the losing teammate would come to Daryl for comfort, and the winning ones would gather for praise.

Daryl's senior year was jubilant. He was captain of a superb team.

Jim and I could follow them all over the area. We loved the tournaments and matches. We yelled until we couldn't speak. I would be so excited I couldn't sleep.

During the wrestling banquets Daryl received many trophies, but "the most valuable wrestler" award was the most sought after.

The coaches and Daryl planned a parents' appreciation night. Rosebuds were ordered for the mothers, refreshments prepared, and special invitations sent.

Before the last match the spotlight was beamed to the center of the gym floor.

The name of the first mother was called. A cheerleader took her by the arm and escorted her to face her son. The son placed a rose in his mother's hand and shook her hand. She returned to her place.

"Mrs. Bullis" was called next. A cheerleader came to my side. I looked across the room to see three cheerleaders with the Bullis boys on their arms. I was sure the girls had drawn straws and this girl at my side had lost. She was to escort me instead of one of the three handsome boys.

Under the spotlight I faced Daryl the pioneer, Bob the Rock of Gibraltar, and Dave the unpredictable pixie. My heart was so full of love for each of them. As Daryl gave me the rose and started to shake my hand, I touched my cheek and whispered, "Son, here."

Daryl gently pecked me on the cheek and smiled as his brothers followed. The rest of the team also imitated his example.

Football was Daryl's second sport. To me it was a useless stacking of human bodies. To Daryl football was exciting. He gave it his all. It had cost him a cartilage in each knee, cuts, and innumerable bruises.

In Daryl's senior year, Bob had said, "Ma, make sure you go to the homecoming game." I tried to find out why, but Bob would say no more.

The first half of the game was over. Daryl was not playing since he had had knee surgery and was still on crutches. It was late in November and very cold. I wished I were home.

The band began to play, interrupting my grumbles to Jim. The announcer delivered the message that this was the Homecoming Game, and that the Depew High School homecoming king and queen would be crowned. Cheerleaders came with the robes and crowns. Beautiful colored flowers were arranged to brighten the dreary November weather. A lovely girl was coaxed from the stands. As she was robed, the audience stood to their feet with claps and cheers.

Once again seated, what Bob had tried to tell me became apparent. I watched as Daryl, on his crutches, was led forth to be the homecoming king. I was the first to my feet with clapping hands and tear-filled eyes. I knew it was Daryl's loving spirit which had given him this honor among his peers.

I prayed from the stands:

O Father, bring him to the greatest coronation when you will present the robe of righteousness and the crown of life.

O Father, who gave David safety in the caves, can you give my children security when we must leave them to follow your call?

12
Rock
of
Gibraltar

Christmas was near. The children were coming from Indiana and Kentucky. I had decided not to get a tree this year since the children were nearly grown.

Early Christmas Eve, Bob and Daryl hit the door. As they came up the steps where they could see into the living room, they asked one question, "Where is the tree?"

Finding a tree late on Christmas Eve, after businesses have closed, is rather impossible. They found a cast-off "tree" from which a smaller tree had been cut from the top. It provoked much laughter and a conference, after which all the boys scurried out. In a short time they returned with the most beautiful tree we have ever had. It was even decorated with icicles. It had been discarded behind the high school. My, how Bob enjoyed this Christmas.

At Christmas we announced we were going to move to the old, drafty house next to the church, and put up for sale the house we had built. Later we would build again, but presently we needed the money for personal and church bills.

That evening we visited our mission pastor's family. They had taken the attic of the house, where the chapel met, and had turned it into a nice kitchen and family room. During the middle of the visit, Bob excused himself and we didn't see him again until one in the morning. Early the same morning he was up and dressed. He came equipped with smile, hammer, saw, level, and nails.

"Bob, where are you going?" I asked.

"Ma, I don't want to tell you now. But you know I'm not doing anything wrong."

"OK," I said. Bob, still grinning, left the house.

My mind went to work. What could he be doing? I knew he was not doing anything wrong. Bob had been "almost" a perfect boy. He had been an unusually happy baby and had grown up to be a model young adult. He was responsible. When he left home for college we knew he would have no problems. I trusted him—what was he doing?

I could stand it no longer; we would go to church to see if he was there. His car was parked in front of the old, drafty house beside the church. This was the house we were returning to. We hurried through the door into the high-ceilinged rooms.

Listening, we heard the "tap, tap" of a hammer from above. We followed its sounds to the attic where we flushed out a grinning Bob with hammer in hand.

"What are you doing?" I cried.

Bob answered, quietly but assuredly, "I'm making myself a room. I'm going to live here."

"Bob, what do you mean? You live at college. Aren't you going back?"

"No, I don't want to go back."

Jim said, "OK, Bob, the decision is yours. If you don't want to go back, we'll enjoy having you at home." Bob enrolled in a state college and made his nest in the upper room.

Three months after Bob had moved home, I found I had cancer. Between school and his job he came daily to visit me in the hospital. Rushing home he helped care for the two foster children and relieved the strain from Jim.

Things don't remain the same. Jim and I felt a definite call to Canada. As visitors, the boys were not allowed to work, so Bob would have to give up his beloved home.

His sister and her husband invited Bob to move near them in Fort Worth, Texas. Later Bob encouraged his older brother, Daryl, and his new wife to set up their home nearby. Next it was brother David and wife whom Bob and the rest of the family helped to get settled.

Bob built without hammer or nails a place for the whole family. In a few months, Tim, the youngest of the Bullis children, will leave Canada for his second home. He will be surrounded by a loving family.

Our greatest fear before our move to Canada was for our children's happiness. We prayed: "Oh, Father, give our children a new home so they will never feel they are being forced from their nest."

I didn't dream God would shape them into a special family, loving and caring for each other.

Christ, who had no home, who had no place to lay your head, thank you for keeping my children with your loving care. You have provided them with a home and a family, when we were called to serve in the opposite direction.

Father, can you help my dear pixie fit his own armor and find his five smooth talents, with which to win victories?

13
——— My Dear Pixie ———

God has a unique sense of humor. He sends to earth a few special pixies.

Wrapped in small packages, angular in body and mischievous in spirit, he unleashes them upon an unsuspecting world.

I have stood many times watching my small-framed son joke and laugh through wrestling matches. His body would bend, curl, turn inside out, creating moves that were never used before and may never be used again. As a result, his statuette form was often displayed on the first-place winners' stand.

We saw him jump from the football stands and take his place by the lovely cheerleaders who were desperately trying to evoke a cheer from a cold crowd. The girls gave him a pom-pom which he took in his left hand. A perfect mirror image of the girls, he led the cheer. The school crowd laughed and cheered loudly with him. A touchdown by our team went unnoticed.

David the pixie, at a very young age, would worm his way into visitors' laps and hearts. He had a talent for knowing the right answers and often the wrong actions.

David was self-reliant and deeply sensitive to others. He of all my children is the least predictable.

We were sitting down for Sunday dinner. I asked, "Where is David?"

A voice from the door said, "Here I am." Later, he laughingly said, "Ma, you left me at church. When you and Dad were gathering the Sunday School children to take them home, I was behind the church playing. You left me, so I hitchhiked home." The six miles for a seven-year-old boy was one of his earliest challenges. Greater ones would come, since he was never in the right place at the right time.

I can almost hear my many calls throughout the years, "David, come and fix this thing." Soon his brothers were saying, "Let Dave fix it—he knows how." David's nimble fingers would go to work, repairing the broken objects. His knowledge of electronics and motors came from taking apart everything he could get his hands on. He had to see what made them tick. Many hours were spent reading encyclopedias, storing up information on many subjects.

Self-confidence seemed to be born in him. His drive to play football with his older brothers put him in the hospital for nine weeks. Older brother Daryl fell on David's leg and broke it above the knee. David was placed in traction and missed half of the school year.

Years later, when David was asked if he had experience in building houses, he said, "Yes, I've helped build two houses." We laughed since he was only four years old when he helped me drive the nails into the floor and pick up scrap lumber to be burned. The next time we built a house, he was eight years old. He was still helping me, driving nails and picking up, but his young mind was trying to take it all in. He was positive he could build a house.

An area in which he had a right to boast of his confidence was cooking and sewing. If Dave needed a patch on his pants, he sewed it on. Anytime we were away on trips, David was the cook for the Bullis boys. He can make biscuits deserving a blue ribbon. We knew the boys would never starve when David was there.

A David has the capacity to be a great missionary, an outstanding preacher, successful con artist, a gun-slinging desperado, or a great adventurer. He is in the process of becoming what God wants him to be.

At seventeen years of age David graduated from high school and was transplanted into the university with his brother, Daryl. Our move to Canada left him without a home, since he couldn't work in Canada. Dave spent several months back in his old Depew home area, attending the home church. This was a time of growth for him in the Lord. While there, David encountered different sects. This demanded some real Bible study to come up with answers. He asked for a Greek New Testament and a concordance. Bible searching has a tendency to make a person grow.

O Father, Saul's armor did not fit young David of old. My David does not fit the design of his brothers. He is a special creation. Help him as he searches out his five smooth talents, and with his sling of determination may he have victories.

May you say that this David is a man after your heart.

14
Tim's Greatest
——————— Undeserved ———————
Punishment

Tim's greatest undeserved punishment didn't occur when his father burst into the kitchen, lifted Tim from his chair, and spanked him. When it was over Tim fought bravely not to cry. The children, seated at the table, stared at their father. Tim's face was clouded with a shocked look—his words unbelieving.

"Daddy, why did you do that?"

"You know, and if you don't, ask your sister. She heard you, too," Jim said angrily.

All eyes turned to Virginia's shocked face. "Daddy, I don't know. Tim did nothing."

We looked at each other. We had just driven up to the front of the house. The warmth of the summer day had wooed open the house's windows. We heard the familiar shrill scream.

"Jim, you must do something about Tim's screaming," I had said. Tim, the youngest, was eleven years old. He couldn't win in direct combat or by his wits, so he screamed. Usually "Ma! Ma! Ma!" got my attention. When Ma was away he just screamed loudly, shrilly, and determinedly. He had been warned.

The unexpected looks caused Jim to continue. "Tim, you cannot go through life . . . " Before he could finish he was interrupted by a loud scream.

This scream came from the house across the street, floating through our living-room windows, across the living room, and into the kitchen where we were standing.

Jim placed his arms around his son's shoulders and looked into his face and said, "Tim, you'll never know how bad I feel. I have made a mistake. I'm sorry!"

Tim's greatest undeserved punishment was imposed on himself. His room became his prison and the walls his boundary. His curtains were drawn; he spent his time alone—watching television and playing "Risk."

He decided, "I will serve my term and then go back to the United States."

Then the day came. Tim's life had been interrupted. For the past ten years he had gone to the same school system, and he had lived in only two houses. Things had been stable and unchanging. He was a Bullis in a school where he and his brothers were well known. Tim was a good wrestler, and his coach had said that by the time Tim was a senior he could be a champion. Before Tim had started the eleventh grade, we moved to the Golden Horseshoe area of Canada.

The summer before, Tim had been allowed to remain in Depew to work at a job since he couldn't work in Canada. When September came—the gates to the states closed—Tim entered his cell. He was robbed of his chance to make good in sports and graduate with his high school class, and he had been plunged into a new world. This new world didn't know him, for he was a stranger in a foreign land. Tim didn't complain, rebel, or argue; he simply placed himself in prison.

He left his prison for a miserable day at school or to help in the new chapel. He was ready to set up chairs and help with young children. His politeness and kindness were pleasing to the adults on Sundays. Back to his shackles he went on Monday. I became very concerned and asked the Father for help.

Pastor Glen Stern, of our mother church in Grove City, Ohio, made it possible for us to have a second car, the brightest Maverick in Burlington.

Tim escaped long enough to practice driving. He found that the car gave him some identity when his license was obtained. With the car he made new friends. He made trips back to his childhood home where things had changed. Old friends find new friends and interests are weaned.

Spring arrived, dressed in its most beautiful cloak. Burlington, located on Lake Ontario, is kept like a lovely park by its residents. Even Tim began to brag about the gorgeous surroundings. Leaving his prison walls, Tim saw our desire was not to shortchange him but to share with him our love for this new area and our desire to do God's will.

Tim, unknowingly, shared with me the key to his cell's door. I read with delight the poem he had placed on his wall:

> We cannot cause the wind to blow
>   the way we want it to,
> but we can so adjust our sails that
>   they will take us where we want to go.
>
> —ANONYMOUS

O Father, the direction in which Tim sets his sails will be in his hands, but Father, please be the captain of his ship.

15
God's
───────Unfailing───────
Clock

In Old Testament days, river paths opened and closed like doors; the sun obediently stood still as a man of God commanded; lifted hands caused battles to be won and when dropped to be lost. Haman built a gallows in time to be hanged from it; a wine taster remembered God's man at a precise moment to change two nations' history; a great fish swam in stormy waters underneath a boat to save Jonah from burial in the sea. The Bible reveals God as he is made real by his unfailing timing.

Does your timing work in answer to prayer?

A man pulled into a restaurant with his head slumped over on the steering wheel. With muffled voice he cried, "Father, send someone to help me—my load is too heavy." Seconds passed, slowly the man straightened up, left his car, and entered the restaurant.

Jim and I, being new to this city, had by faith rented a school building for future worship services. Now we were heading home. Without a comment, Jim swung his car into the same parking lot. We hurried in, asked for salad plates, stopped for our beverage, and met the man who earlier cried to the Lord for help. While he paid his bill, the cashier reached beneath the counter, saying, "Sir, you left this book when you were here the last time." It was the man's well-worn Bible.

"That's a great book," Jim said. "I have 5,000 portions of Luke/Acts in my living room and 1,000 copies of *Good News for Modern Man* stacked up waiting for our move here."

"You're Christians?" the man asked. "Do you mind if I eat with you?"

As we ate the man revealed his many concerns. All of us rejoiced that we were moving to this city, we prayed, thanking God for His answers to burdens even as we carried them.

Our new friend exclaimed, "Isn't it wonderful that God can work in mini-seconds? If I had come earlier or later, we would've missed this time together. God, knowing I needed to talk to someone, brought you on his exact schedule."

After our move our new friend came back to the area on business and called us.

"Hello. This is Mary Bullis."

"It's really you? I didn't think anyone would answer. I had decided God had sent two angels just when I needed them. It seemed beyond logic to believe God had answered my needs."

I liked being called an angel—God's messenger. Yet, as Jim and I had fellowship with him, his happy conversation revealed how glad he was that we were flesh and blood.

God, can you lift our eyes to see the unlikely?

I never drive from the Pennsylvania entrance of the New York Throughway without thinking of God's timing. We were moving from Ohio to New York. My mother and I were transporting our car to the new field while Jim was driving the rental truck and my father was driving Daryl and Bob. We had been separated by the miles and the beautiful scenery of this new area. Father hadn't been given the new address so I could only hope that he was following Jim's truck.

I noticed the sign announcing a rest stop at Angola. Virginia was gawking at the pedestrian crosswalk over the expressway, carrying hungry travelers from either side to the restaurant.

"Mom!" cried Virginia. "There's Grandpa . . . Daryl . . . and I see Bob." I looked up and there they stood above our heads, watching the cars go underneath them. I swung the car into the right lane and exited directly beyond the walkway. We hurried up the ramp to find them and travel the rest of the trip together.

A minute or two one way or the other . . .

When the dark periods come, can we see God's goodness from the end of the tunnel?

On Wednesday after school started, I was busy in the house when I heard a call.

"Ma, come quick! David's hurt!"

I hurried from the house to the park where David was lying on the ground. My eyes quickly examined him and found no spilled blood. He was awake and joking. I thought, *Oh, thank God! He isn't hurt badly.*

Jim called for an ambulance. Daryl, the oldest brother, remorsefully related the story. He and Dave had jumped towards the football, but Daryl, who was seventy-five pounds heavier, carried Dave to the ground.

"Ma, I heard his leg snap like a tree limb. We told him not to move, but . . . he's hurt real bad!"

The police immediately came from across the street. The ambulance attendants immobilized David's leg with an air cast and we were on our way to the hospital.

I reassured myself that it was only a broken leg and that as soon as he had a permanent cast we would be on our way home. Nothing could hold energetic David down. To my disbelief David did not come home right away. They put a pin through his knee and suspended his leg under traction. David, who had not been a good student, would lose a semester of school. How could he contain his nervous energy? How would this prolonged stay affect him?

Jim tutored him. The nurses enthroned him and entertained him lavishly, taken by his boyish charm. I'm a mama talking. David and I spent enjoyable mornings together as I came to visit him each weekday.

Fifty days later, on Wednesday before Thanksgiving, the doctor said David could go home. At the church Thanksgiving dinner David was the star attraction, and from Thanksgiving until after Christmas he recuperated. With school reopening in January he was eager to return. To our joy he didn't have to repeat the term he missed; rather his learning ability had increased, his desire to achieve had heightened, and his reading had so improved that he would enjoy it for the rest of his life. All things had worked together for good.

We were thankful for our insurance company for they paid most of the hospital bill. But when the final bill came we knew it was impossible for us to pay. We were still in the midst of a bleak, worrisome tunnel.

God's timing is unique, for in Orrville, Alabama, lives a Christian farmer, Carl Henderson. For some reason Carl sent an unexpected check to James Bullis to be used as he saw fit, with the check arriving the same week as the hospital bill. God's timing works!

God, who guides the weather fronts, can you control the collisions of humanity's courses?

"I came to know the Lord by accident!" a tall, grey-haired man testified.

"I remember the day I jumped into my car parked in the driveway. Looking in both directions, I backed into the street. Now in my haste I didn't see the car backing out of a driveway just across the street. The minor crash caused an awkward blocking of the street.

"The other driver, a red-haired man, climbed from his car to face me. Many drivers get out cursing and blaming the other driver. He wasn't what I had expected.

" 'Looks like we didn't see each other,' he softly spoke with a smile. An examination of the damages showed that he had some, while my car seemed to have none.

" 'You take care of your car,' he suggested. 'I'll take care of mine. By the way, I'm Jim Bullis, the pastor of the Southern Baptist Church in town, and I'd like to visit you and share the beautiful story of Christ.' A time was decided on, and I went on to work.

"When Pastor Bullis arrived for the visit, I heard the good news of salvation and eagerly trusted Christ. Later I followed the Lord in baptism, becoming a member of the church.

"I know it was God's perfect timing which brought our paths together, giving the message of salvation to me. Oh, yes! I found Christ *by accident.*"

God, can you delay that which would harm us until . . . we can better deal with it?

After a summer with no spare time, God allowed a catastrophe. We had been hosting ten summer missionaries, several Christian Service Corps workers, but we had only our one car. The summer was past, the Bible Schools finished, and the day camp closed down. The missionaries had just left the day before, and we were anticipating a weekend of recuperation.

So, Bob was carefully driving the family car while I relaxed beside him. One of his friends sat in the back seat. Bob pulled into the left-turn lane of a wide street, made a proper turn signal, and patiently waited for a lull in the oncoming traffic.

Brakes squealed. We braced ourselves as we were rammed from

behind. The wide, empty road had become a funnel for the two inebriated young men in their unlicensed car. Our car's rear bumper was crammed just below the rear window. It sat high upon an unruptured gas tank, and wheels and springs were twisted downward like kangaroo legs holding us aloft. We found safety in its inner pocket. No one was injured!

Now we had *no* car! Yet, if the wreck had been a month, a week, or even a couple of days earlier . . . We were thankful the summer program was over and there was time to find another auto. We rented a car to begin our search of local and distant lots and car ads in the newspapers. The finance company ended up with all but four hundred dollars of the settlement, which made our search hopeless. The price of old, but passable, cars was over a thousand dollars. We went farther and farther afield, but received only amused smirks at our quest for a four-hundred-dollar car.

After a long morning of searching, Jim drove by an automobile repair garage. He dejectedly stopped and asked the Jewish owner, who had been helpful in the past, if he had a car under four hundred dollars. The man grinned and answered:

"Rev. Ike (his nickname for Jim), I wouldn't sell you a car. All mine are junk and besides you're too hard on any car. I value your friendship. Let me see . . . today is Wednesday. Today at 1 PM in Batavia they're having a police car auction. If you leave right now you can make it, and I'm sure you will find your car."

Jim rushed to our rented car shouting his thanks and we started the hour drive to Batavia. There the cars sat all in a row. Some were wrecked, others had motor or transmission problems, and some seemed in tip-top shape. We just knew our four hundred dollars couldn't buy one of the latter. Our time was short, and a decision about which car to bid on had to be made. The auctioneer adjusted his microphone. He tested it a few times, giving us extra minutes. Quicky we agreed on a baby-blue Plymouth.

Looking around we saw other buyers who seemed to know what they were doing—dealers who were there to buy low and sell high and mechanics who were seeking car parts. All of them seemed so experienced, while we stood there realizing we were novices without enough cash.

The auctioneer explained the rules. The first was no checks would be accepted. Our hearts sank. The gravelly voice of the auctioneer chanted. Soon "our" Plymouth was being driven to the crowded viewing ground. The bidding began. Jim tried not to look anxious. After all, if Jesus could know the fish which contained the needed tax coins, he knew which car our few dollars could buy.

"One hundred!" The bidding commenced.

The auction sluggishly continued, climbing twenty or twenty-five dollars at a time. It finally stood at three hundred and seventy-five dollars.

"Who will give $400?" called the auctioneer.

"I'll give $400," offered Jim.

"Who will give $420?"

Knowing if the challenge were taken, we could go no higher, we waited breathlessly.

"Going once . . . ?"

"Going twice . . . ?"

"And sold!"

It was over. Jim walked to the pay window with his check. The lady there looked at it and explained slowly and surely that they did not take checks. Then with a grin she said:

"Reverend, it had better be good."

It took two weeks to make all the necessary arrangements, but the car came to stay at the Bullis's home. It proved to be a car which God knew would not die. After 125,000 miles we retired it as a rusted, collision-sculptured friend with bald tires.

God's goodness through a Jewish friend ushered us to the right place on the one day of the year when we could have found our car. A tribe of police cars carried our family the next few years.

Can you control all things, as you did Peter's fishing nets and the fish in the sea below, to bring in a large catch?

It was to be a Christmas wedding at the Veteran's Park Baptist Church. It was the church's first large wedding, and an event which would interest the whole Frontier Baptist Association. From Orchard Park to Niagara Falls, from Batavia to the Niagara River, people were coming to see our daughter, the bride, for she had lived in the area since she was nine.

The wedding dress was completed and the announcements were mailed. The bridesmaids had accepted their invitations of honor, and the groom had chosen his best man and groomsmen who were coming from the Midwest.

I, mother of the bride, was busy with the final details. My monetary needs were growing daily. The list included: flowers for the church, participants, and decorations; candles and decorations purchased to enhance the service; special food for the rehearsal dinner and reception; gifts; film and bulbs for the volunteer photographer; my dress and Jim's suit cleaned, and more. This was complicated by four boys looking for gifts during the Christmas season.

The father of the bride, Jim, was busy too. He was trying to put together the events which had carried him to this place. His mind clung to God's perfect timing when less than twenty days before Christmas he had sold several buses. God was giving us the necessary wedding money. Within ample time the church purchasing the buses had sent drivers to drive them back South. They assured Jim they would wire the commission to his bank account since they had not brought a check to reimburse him. Jim had promised the money to bride, mother, and boys.

During the next few days Jim returned constantly to the promises of God. He knew Jesus enjoyed weddings. God's timing was perfect. God never fails. He called the church repeatedly, also the bank and wire services, for evidence of the missing money. It had been swallowed up in a vast unconcerned wire labyrinth.

God was in control, so Jim felt he should give it a few more days. December 21 brought my parents for the holiday festivities including the wedding. But the money still eluded us. The urgency forced Jim to recall all the groups involved. The sluggish search meandered through the complicated chain of financial institutions. Jim decided to start at the New York City offices of the two large banks concerned. Speaking to the bored voice in their wire-service department, he shared his problem:

"I must locate my money. My children will have no Christmas. Worst of all, I will have a church full of people and no flowers, candles, food, or cake for my daughter's wedding. Can you tell me where to search next?"

The reply was filled with evasiveness and warnings that the Christmas parties were in full force. This was the wrong time of the year to get anything done. However, they did promise the money would be found *after* the holiday season.

Jim hung up the phone, and for the next twenty minutes he sat waiting impatiently. We still knew the prodigal money must come home.

The phone rang, and he was informed the money had been located and was being forwarded. It had been routed to the wrong city. I suppose this was one of the most nerve-wracking situations we have ever faced. Yet, it was replaced at the beautiful, unruffled wedding as every candle, flower, snapped picture, and guest spoke of the presence of Him whose first ministry honored a wedding.

Jesus knew every line of the computerized wire system.

Thank you, Father of ages and eons, for directing my seconds, hours, and days. Your timing gives what is best for my life.

16
Death
———— in the ————
Parsonage

Thanksgiving Day balkingly refused to pass for our disturbed neighbors. They had badgered the windows and worried the house, trying to discover the secrets so well-kept from their probing eyes.

It began when the police car, with its penetrating lights, called attention to our driveway. Our solemn faces were noticed by the household next door. Something had happened!

The parade increased with a second car—a plain, black car with a symbol glaring at the beholders with the words, "The Coroner's Office." Our house was bathed in a strange wave of eerie silence.

The family car was almost missed as it pulled away from the house. The darting eyes were like minnow nets, trying to capture the faces of those who had been in the car. There had been four, red-haired boys filling the seats and windows, their large eyes still tied to their house behind them. The boys had a look of fright and unhappiness, which seems to be best mirrored in the eyes of children.

The women's search missed the embarrassed figure of the teenage girl who was drawn down as if to become a part of the interior of the car. She wanted no trespassing on her world by the ones who lived around her. She was somehow angered by the events that had made Thanksgiving Day a period of regret and unhappiness.

Virginia's mind was filled with death and its surprising visit in a world which she could not understand. She was facing a time of searching.

A hearse, made larger by its attached fears, crept up to the door and cut off the direct vision of the two neighbors who by now were facing the sadness of death in the preacher's home. Their tears were beginning to flow.

The white of the sheet was perfect for masking the form of the covered body. The wide-open mouth of the hearse slowly and completely swallowed up the stretcher. Then it was closed, and the hearse soon slipped out of sight.

They watched as Pastor Jim walked out to the bus alone. Their eyes tried to find the slight figure of the daughter of the family. The church bus roared into action. On the face of the pastor who drove it, they saw unhappiness and deep sorrow. They had an answer to the riddle.

The daughter, Virginia, had died.

Others on the street talked about the passing of Virginia. They wondered how a family could cope with such a turmoil on this Thanksgiving day.

Caged as they were by their pride in not minding other people's business, they waited with intense anxiety. Finally the bus and car pulled back into the yard. The bus blocked the vision of the neighbors from seeing the young frame of the active daughter as she hurried into the house.

The doors of uncaring were done away with. They had to make some gesture of human concern. The neighbor's daughter said to her mother, "I know the pastor's daughter is dead. I must go and see them."

She came with the rusing of a determined mind. She called through the screen into the darkness, "Mary, is Virginia all right?"

Virginia came and stood before her. Her words, springing from the release of fears, tumbled out, "Oh, thank God, you're alive!"

She came inside on weakened legs and sat at our table as I shared the past week's events.

The week began with a World Missions Conference in one of the southern states. I went on my yearly journey to help make the southern part of the nation aware of the needs of the pioneer areas of the North. It had been a joy to share the work of my church and its wonderful people.

I had called home just before my flight to tell Jim all was well. He had shared the fact that he had a surprise. He had invited a guest to stay with us for awhile. My heart sank for I knew of Jim's guests. The story was not to be any different from others of the past. The guest was the father of some children he had met in his Vacation Bible School. They were now riders on his bus to Sunday School. As they entered the bus they had told him their father was in the Veterans' Hospital because of his alcoholism.

Pastor Jim decided to visit the man in the hospital. The patient's wife had informed him that her husband could not return home. She said her husband's drinking had destroyed her's and the children's lives—it had to end. She had brought him clean clothes and said she loved him. She tried to care for his needs, but their lives had to be free of his drink.

He was deeply depressed since he had no place to go when ready to leave the hospital.

Jim gave him the gospel message which presented the man a glimmer of hope, but it was not accepted. Jim decided to bring him home with the prayer that the glimmer would become the dawning of the Morning Star of promise and give new life to his friend and death to the old, drunken life-style.

It was Wednesday morning. We were just getting up when we were told by our guest that it was paycheck day. He was to sign up at the unemployment office and get a check. We dropped him off, and upon returning we found the place vacant.

Frantic calls from his mother revealed him to have fallen captive to his thirst in a local drinking trap. My husband, armed with his determination and prayer, walked in and dragged him out of the joint. Jim was sickened by the uncaring of the people who were watching a life being destroyed.

In order to keep him in sight, Jim took him along to make the day's business stops. He visited a government office on some bus business. Our guest was given black coffee and a place in the air-conditioned waiting room of the government office. Buffalo's bars and taverns drew our guest away from the place of safety. He was gone less than ten minutes after Jim stepped through the door of the adjoining offices.

We sat by the telephone eager to hear from our guest. At 11:30 the silence of the long evening was broken by the ring of the telephone. It was the hospital asking if Jim could come for our guest. They said he was drunk. My husband left to pick him up.

I pulled the turkey from the oven to carve it for Thanksgiving dinner. It was a festive time of the year.

The time for Jim to come home soon doubled and tripled. The telephone rang again. It was our friend with a trembling and very defeated voice. The hospital was pushing him to go home. Jim had not arrived yet, and the man was sick. He asked when Jim was coming.

"Stay there," I said. "Jim will soon by there. Something has happened, but he will come. You must. . . . " The phone was soon playing the sound of a lost line.

Forty-five minutes later a car was heard driving into our driveway. The picture window splashed its image on the opposite wall. I saw at a glance a white light on the top of the car. Could it be the police?

I confronted the erring one and a taxi driver at the screen door.

"Lady, he's in a bad way. He said you would pay me."

Shock cut through me. I looked at the man who was telling me to pay. Money at a time like this was harder to find than a snake's lips.

"That will be eleven dollars."

A battered wallet was resigned to me as our drunk friend headed for his room. The four dollars it surrendered increased my panic. A thorough search of my purse, piggy banks, and drawers eked out the required treasure.

The cab driver, with a friendly good-bye, reminded me, "He is really soused. He's in a bad way." After the driver left, the walls seemed different. They had gained a frightening quality. They caged my children and me in with a man who had seemed angry. I looked at the door and listened for haltering footsteps. I knew alcohol could do strange things to any person. I prayed that he would pass into a stupor and wished Jim was at home.

Fifteen minutes later the car drove into the driveway. Jim was covered with dirt. He had had a flat tire downtown with no spare. He had been in the slum area, and only one station was open after midnight. This station was guarded by a big German police dog, showing his pedigreed white teeth.

The keeper of the station was playing cards, which had prevented his closing early. The man stopped the card game. They put their strong hands to work on my husband's bald tires. They laughed at a preacher with no money for spares, who would drive late at night in the unsafe area and cross into the slum part of town.

Jim rolled the tire back to the car. The Plymouth hadn't been vandalized while he was away. He changed the tire and continued the search for his friend. Finally defeated he returned home.

"Mary, is he here?"

"Yes, he's asleep in his room."

Jim went down to check on his friend. He lay there fully clothed, with his shoes still on his feet and his hand over his eyes. Jim tried to get him to talk, but thought the unanswered questions were the result of the man's shame.

In spite of the lack of answers, Jim removed his guest's shoes and socks. As he did so he said, "Never mind, my friend, we shall see victory in the morning." Covering him with a quilt, Jim left the room. The room was dark since he had not turned on the light.

Morning came with all of its comforts. The rest of the night covers the needs and fears of the day before. It has the ability to bring hope back to life, as nothing else can do. Even the body must die a little every night in sleep before it is ready to meet the duties of the next day.

We dressed. The children were dressed. Breakfast was on the table, but our guest had not come upstairs.

Down the same stairs to the room Jim hurried. Our friend still lay in the same pose as the night before. His hand was still covering his eyes, and the quilt was neatly pulled around him.

Jim called me into the room. I reached for the man's hand to pull it from his eyes. He never spoke. His hand resisted my efforts and snapped back into place.

Jim called the police, and I took the children to church for Thanksgiving Day service and dinner. Jim would join us when he could.

Tim, our eight-year-old son said, "Mom, is he really D.E.E.D?" His young mind was trying to understand this new development. His older sister automatically corrected his spelling, "No, Tim, he is D.E.A.D."

"Can I see him?" Daryl asked. "I've never seen a dead man." It was not for their eyes to see. Nor for their hearts to understand why death comes to a thirty-seven-year-old man because he was not willing to reach out for the glimmer of light which could have given him abundant life instead of death and hell.

My young neighbor had listened quietly. As her strength returned, she looked about the room and said, "This doesn't look like a place where a man has just died."

She hurried home to tell her mother the story. "The girl next door didn't die, she's still alive." This soon became the talk of the street.

After the young neighbor left, I looked around the room at my family. I thanked God that we had never faced the sting of death, and that when we would, it would be swallowed up in victory. How I wished Jim's friend could have seen victory that day.

Dear Father, I thank you that we can wait upon you when the unexpected days come.

O Father, who gave Jacob a rock for a pillow which kept him awake so he could see heavenly activities, can you help us accept our rock pillows that we may see heaven's activities? And rename our place of difficulties the house of God?

17
Sharp Stones
——————and——————
Rock Pillows

It's difficult to face our stones and hard pillows until we can look past them and see God's glory. Some of our small irritants (small stones) and large crises (hard pillows) are: weather; religious majorities; culture and language; and loneliness.

WEATHER. It was hard for our family to get used to. The place for ice was in the refrigerator or in ice tea, but not on the roads for most of our driving days. Jim has slid into many small accidents going around slippery corners, stopping on icy streets while approaching a light, causing his "non-cancellable" insurance policy to be cancelled.

The cold has sent us skyrocketing utility bills. The cost of lighting, butane for cooking, oil for heating has been magnified by a drafty old house, pressuring us with astronomical bills. It would have been cheaper to rent a newer house but . . .

Early each winter Jim would start fussing about the hated winter. So, after being in New York state four or five winters, I was shocked when Jim entered the next without a fuss. He laughed after he slipped on the ice or when the frigid, creeping blight reached a two-foot coverage. He fell and injured his coccyx as he was pushing our car from a snowdrift, but he still didn't complain. I asked him what had happened. He stood looking out at the "Winter Wonderland" and said, "This is the day the Lord hath made!"

Learning to cope with frozen steps (small stones) and the high costs (rock pillows) open the windows of heaven where God's glory can be enjoyed.

RELIGIOUS MAJORITIES. At first they were the most intense rock pillow. Being the first Southern Baptists in the area, we found that the other "brands" of Baptists were often afraid in two extreme directions we were either "snake handlers" or "modernists." The predominant religious group (Catholic) had their own ideas about this strange family which moved into the center of their community. It is best illustrated by the following occurrence.

Jim and the boys were cleaning the snow from the walks when the oldest local leader of the Catholic church came by. He looked at our church and our house next door, then at Jim, and muttered. "Yew nudd'n, Yewr built'n nudd'n. Yew work 'ike a Lab'dor!"

Jim understood the man was saying that our work, our building, and Jim himself were nothing. Jim looked at the old man and smiled, saying, "I love this town, and I know we'll see it learn to love us."

The man surveyed Jim's worn coat and his older car sitting by the street and said, "Yewn become Cad-o-lic. Cad-o-lic lay priest can be marrick (married)."

So the community greeted our first efforts. Yet, years later a young community worker approached the police to find churches willing to help in the community youth project. The officer pointed across the street to our small Baptist church as one of the two he recommened as caring.

Another time a group of schoolchildren were on a field trip to the police station. They asked the officer where he sent people in need of food or a place to stay. The policeman answered, "We call the Baptist church 'cause they're concerned.

In the third year of our stay on the Eastern side of Buffalo, the Catholic educational director called our church to find where we obtained our copies of *Good News for Modern Man*. One of the pastors of our churches provided 250 copies for this Catholic Saturday morning religion class. We were privileged to share our abundance with our Catholic friends.

We attended our first of many sports banquets of the community public high school. The master of ceremonies at the banquet was a Polish coach who was also a priest. The total atmosphere of the evening was one which could certainly be appreciated by the Catholic audience. Many kind words were spoken in behalf of the school's football coach which he certainly deserved. He was highly praised for his attendance of mass every weekday morning. The speech was about the rivalry between the Italian Catholics and the Polish Catholics. None felt it was out of place for most everyone there was Catholic.

As this local legend recognized each football player on his team, he spoke a few words as he presented their trophies. As he presented Daryl's and Bob's he lovingly commented:

"These are the *Baptist* boys. They will mean much in our sports program."

Later at Daryl's graduation the coach said to us: "Daryl is a wonderful young man," and laughingly added, "even if he is a Baptist. He is the kind of boy any man would want his son to be."

The "Baptist boys" tag was a hard pillow for our boys who listened to the "Hail Marys" before every game.

During our ten years of service in the Depew community of western New York, our lives were intertwined with the sports life of the high school. Jim was asked to pray at their banquets, often at graduation, and was asked by another school's sports leader to help him write a prayer for a wedding.

We were called to a new place of service, and one final prayer at our sport's banquet was requested. During the presentation of awards, Jim was called forward and given his only trophy, a wall plaque engraved with:

REV. JAMES BULLIS
FOR
INSPIRATION AND DEDICATED
SERVICE TO THE YOUTH OF
OUR COMMUNITY.

A field which is nearly 95 percent Catholic is certainly a religious majority, and provides many stones and pillows of rock. Those stones and pillows help keep us awake, seeking the activity of God's hand, bringing joy as we learn to live with and love these people—and to be loved in return.

Another small irritatant was finding that the common things of the South had become either unknown, unacceptable, or even exotic. During a series of "foreign" meals our church sponsored to attract prospects, we were nonplussed by the people's choice—the "strangest meal."

It was not a Chinese meal; not a meal prepared by Polish cooks; not a German repast; not Italian pasta. These were ordinary, but the Southern home-cooked meal was a new experience to the majority.

Their comments were:

"So this is corn bread. I thought it was cake. Can I eat it with the food?"

"Pinto beans—I never tasted beans like these."

"Barbecued chicken—It's good but we never fix our chicken like this."

"Banana pudd'n—It's the best dessert I've ever tasted!"

The differences in food changed from a small stone to adventures in learning. Have you ever had "duck-blood soup?" We did! The life and lore of the South did have a pull upon us but we had no desire to look back. Lot's wife turned to salt, but if we had looked back, we would have simply grown stale or gone back home. There can be no looking back!

The large stone of language shrank to pebble size. Had we gone to the Catholic land of Colombia, South America, we would have had to spend many nights upon the rock of language. But God knew best and sent us from Missouri, one of the "You'uns" states, to Texas, one of the "ya'll" states, later to New York, the "Youse guys" state, and lastly to the Canadian-English, "all of you."

The pebbles of language enhanced laughter in Ohio. We were puzzled when the neighborhood child stood on our doorstep and asked in one short breath: "Plice-Daryl-loud-out?" (meaning, "Please, is Daryl allowed out?")

In New York we ate "pēcan pie."

In Ontario the man in the post office asked, "How you been keeping, eh?" (Translation: "How are you today?") I looked twice when I was asked to have a seat on the "Chesterfield" (couch).

Some pioneer pastors from the Deep South have to face a larger language problem, especially if they have older children. One of these families had taught their children to answer all adults with, "Yes Ma'am" and "Yes Sir." The schoolteacher sent home a note demanding the children stop using those phrases. The highly upset mother called the teacher to ask what was wrong with being polite? The words of the teacher shocked her: "Nothing. That is a virtue. Yet, with your children's politeness and their strong regional accent they combine to cause undue teasing from their peers." Irritating!

Our first summer in Canada, a young summer missionary from the Deep South came back in tears, saying:

"These here folks air the most im-po-lité pe-oṕ-le Ah 'ave evuh seen."

We laughed and explained they were not making fun of her because she was telling them about Christ, but they were enjoying her "Suthun" accent. The clipped-speech Canadians were hearing the honeyed tones of the magnolia trees on their front doorsteps. Many of them were hearing it for the first time.

The young missionary went back out and outperformed herself for such an appreciative audience. Their laughter had become applause as she shared the message of Christ.

For some, the largest and most uncomfortable rock of all was that of loneliness. On this rock many pioneer pastors have floundered and returned to their homes. Learning to cope with this barrier saves a person from much heartbreak.

This rock was not a large one for me—in fact, it was a pebble while we were in Ohio and New York.

My husband, Jim, is my best friend. Together we anticipated many adventures. I am one half and he's the other. Our lives were so complete we could both leave our families, cleaving together to cope with new problems in new regions. I could cry on his shoulder—he on mine. We agreed not to be discouraged at the same time. If he were under pressure, I prayed: "God, help me make it easier for Jim." When things were bad for me, Jim held my hand and shared my load.

To work effectively in a pioneer area your husband/wife must be your best friend.

Our house with its five children, at times foster children, neighborhood children, and church children made it almost impossible to be by yourself, let alone be lonely. Yet, if your husband, your children, and you are not a close unit, friction and strain develop. In a pioneer mission field the greatest strength is the home. All else is in the embryonic stage, church, Christian friends, and respect.

This is best expressed by what happened to Tim when he was young.

Jim had gone out to see if he could save on our grocery bill. He went to a large warehouse and asked about damaged goods. The warehouseman took him to a back room and showed him barrels filled with cans.

Some were bent almost to a "C" shape; others were crushed, spilling their contents; some were without labels. He took them all! Phew! Ugh! THANK you, LORD!

We were amazed when Jim returned with the station wagon filled with cans from five trash barrels for almost nothing. Did we find a great variety in his bargain? No, but we were thankful that we liked tomato soup (one fourth of the cans). There were also cans of dog food, cat food, beans, and beets.

The most precious were the cans of asparagus. They were a special treat because the price prohibited their purchase in a regular store. We all loved the cans of green delight, except Tim.

One night, the asparagus was served with a meat loaf, potatoes, and salad for supper. As I opened one can of asparagus, I noticed a few small bubbles. I asked Jim to taste it, and together we agreed that it was a boon from God, manna for pennies.

After the short blessing, the asparagus disappeared, with no help from young Tim. While I walked to the cabinet for the cake I looked at Virginia and David. Both looked a little white around the lips. Food goes through Jim quickly—he was headed for the bathroom. Soon, it was evident we had a touch of food poisoning.

As Tim looked from one of us to the other his eyes were filled with empathy, for he was not sick. No asparagus had passed his lips. His young mind must have thought what if something bad happened to his family. He would be alone.

He watched as Jim dialed the emergency department of the hospital to ask the results of eating "bad" asparagus. Before the doctor on call could answer, Tim with quivering voice said: "Ma, if you are all going to die and go to heaven, I don't want to be left alone. Have you got a couple of spoonfuls of asparagus left?"

I crushed him in my arms and assured him I was positive nothing bad was going to happen. Jim repeated the doctor's message, saying it would not seriously harm us except to give us diarrhea.

Tim's response was my assurance—the pebbles of loneliness were nothing as long as we had each other. We were certainly a family of oneness.

The third reason my loneliness amounted only to pebbles was the friendship we had with our associational directors of missions and their wives. Many years ago when we were new to missions, Associational

Missions Director Dick Carlton and his wife of Cincinnati, Ohio, shared with us their knowledge of mission Bible School work. Charles Magruder and Eva stood by our side and gave us a vision of starting new chapels in Western New York. Ellis Turner and Eloise were our beloved missionaries during hard times. Brother and Mrs. Clifford Matthews came to Buffalo, New York, just before we moved, and we admired their unending zeal. Loneliness was impossible when there was such good leadership.

What took the edge from the pebble called loneliness was the *koinonia* of fellow pastors and wives at our side. These men and women shared our vineyard. There was the Porters' inspiration by their faithful service which has built a strong church; Charles and Loretta Johnson who bought a huge church building in a small town, and have worked diligently to fill it; Byron and Judy Lutz who have been our special friends over the years. Our mission pastors and their wives were "our support." How we loved Curtis and Jackie Monday, Gilmore and Ruth Samuelson, and big, lovable Ralph and miniature Shirley Fingerlow. The list goes from one end of the Frontier Association to the other over the years. We stood together in love and fellowship.

The associational functions were a support to me. Training, edification, and fellowship were the ladders by which God's messengers gave us encouragement and strength. John and Doris Tubbs gave tremendous leadership. The associational program is one of the greatest strengths of Southern Baptists.

My church family came one by one, filling my life. The rock of loneliness was exchanged for arms of living, loving people. One of God's greatest promises will always be that "where two or three are gathered in my name, there I will be in their midst." The strength of the two or three, plus Christ, leaves no room for loneliness.

Earlier I commented that there was never a rock of loneliness in Ohio and New York, only pebbles. But in July 1979, when we moved across Lake Ontario to Burlington, Ontario, I found not a pebble of loneliness—but a large stone pillow.

Why the change with only a move across a lake?

My best friend and husband, Jim, and I were ahead of time. The things which had kept us from loneliness before were not with us anymore.

Our children couldn't move with us, except for Tim who had two years before he would be gone. How I missed them all!

There was no associational missionary, for we were the first Southern Baptists in the Golden Horseshoe area. Every pastor needs an associational missionary. There was no associational missionary's wife to understand my needs. How empty!

No fellow "Southern Baptist pastors" and wives to march beside us. We invited the pastors and wives of the Baptist groups of our area into our home. It was good to have their fellowship, but we missed those driven by the same mission desire and evangelistic thrust. We missed those who marched to the same drum of missions, the Cooperative Program, associational missions, Miss Lottie, Miss Annie, and denominational-sponsored home and foreign missions. These are the things which make our pulse beat with the same fervor.

As I lie on my large rock pillow of loneliness in Ontario, Canada, I see the activities of heaven. I feel the surging call of men and women, missionaries and pastors, to add their labor to those already here. With their coming, my rock pillow will become a pebble.

O Father, who gave Jacob a special rock for a pillow to keep him awake that he might see heavenly activities, thank you for my sharp stones and rock pillow, that I may see the heavens open and many messengers climbing to build your place of worship.

Lord, over all who call upon him, "how then shall they call on him in whom they have not believed? And how shall they believe in him of whom they have not heard? And how shall they hear without a preacher? And how shall they preach, except they be sent?" (Rom. 10:14-15).

18
Glad Tidings
of
Good Things

"Oh, Father, many of these little ones have never heard a Bible story. Most may never hear another Bible story. Help me to tell this story as if it were the last one they will ever hear. Father, help me make it a story of Jesus which they will never forget. Amen."

I remember praying this life-changing prayer during my second summer in Western New York. I had been asked to help in a Bible school in the community building of the Sheridan Park area.

The first day I had twenty-nine children from grades one to three. Tomorrow, the number would double, so I asked Mrs. Eva Magruder, the wife of the director of missions, to help.

There were forty-nine the second day. Using tables to divide the room, she took one half and I the other. During that week the total enrollment numbered one hundred and twenty-five!

One morning I faced about forty children sitting on the floor around me. Some had come in play clothes, some in swimming suits, and one in his pajamas.

I asked, "How many of you don't have a Bible at home?" So many hands went up, I thought they didn't understand my Southern drawl. I repeated it more slowly and very clearly. Still the hands went into the air around me.

Looking at the eyes of these young children I saw pools of emptiness waiting to be filled. I saw hearts that would become dirty with sin unless they learned of Christ's cleansing power. I saw hands that would belong to Satan unless Christ captured them. Tears came into my eyes.

A choir group came from the South. They stood before another group of children on the eastern side of Buffalo. Their leader said, "OK, you all know John 3:16. Let's say it together." The leader expected great participation. They started, "For God so loved. . . . " The leader stopped. Only the youth workers from the South were repeating the verse.

A young mother was given a Bible by her mother-in-law. During a visit the young mother brought her Bible to show me how much she had read. I knew she was busy since she had two small children. The books she had read were marked. They included Genesis through Proverbs, one half of the Old Testament. But, no one had ever told her where the stories of Christ could be found.

We opened the Gospels and took a pencil, marking the plan of salvation. At the end she asked Christ to come in and give her new life.

But how can they understand if they have not heard?

My bus route was in the mission area twelve miles from our church. I went to visit at the Wilson home. Mrs. Wilson was a friendly woman with three daughters. A few months later two of her daughters attended a Bible school at our camp land. During the week, in the afternoon, Jim was driving his old car in front of their house when it gave a jerk and died.

As he stood by the car, he thought, *Lord, I don't have time for this. Why did it have to stop now?* A cheery voice came from the yard nearby, "Hello, Pastor." It was one of the Wilson twins who had been in Bible School. She volunteered to get her sister and mother to help shove the car into their driveway. Mrs. Wilson added that her husband could get it running.

On Saturday, when Jim went to pick the car up, he asked to share with them a message they had never heard before. Jack Wilson was curious to see the man who claimed to be a minister and drove such a dismal wreck. Upon entering the room, Jim was offered the husband's chair. Just as Mrs. Wilson warned, "Pastor, don't lean! . . . " Jim eased back into the chair and his head went back while his feet stuck straight up into the air.

Since Jim is a good-sized person it took all of them to right the chair amid the general laughter.

Jim then gave the Wilsons their first Bible. They opened the Scriptures, and during the next hour and a half, Jim shared Christ's message of salvation. All prayed asking Christ to be the Lord of their lives. Jim later baptized them. He said, "These are the first members of the Alden Baptist Chapel."

How can they call on him whom they have not heard?

Barbara Wilson's brother, Herm, was extremely close to the family, and Jack and Herm were partners. Herm and his wife, Pat, recognized the change in their relatives.

One day Jack and Herm were playing pool. When they played, Herm always won. After a few games Jack said, "Herm, if I win, will you go to church with me?"

Herm laughed and, feeling it was a sure thing, said, "Yes, Jack, if you win, I'll go to church with you."

The next Sunday, Herm kept his promise and came to church. Jack knew the Lord must have helped him win since he certainly could not have won by himself.

Jim was invited to a Bible study at the home of Herm and Pat. After going through the plan of salvation they joined their hands in prayer. Herm accepted Christ. He said it was the greatest experience of his life, feeling the Spirit while they prayed. Pat later came to the Lord, and they were baptized. The Alden Baptist Chapel was started in their home. By simply sharing her faith Barbara saw eighteen members of her family saved.

How shall they believe in him whom they have not heard?

A friend said, "My mother lives in your area, but she won't go to church." We made the visit and found a shy little woman living alone, rarely leaving her house. Her shyness kept her from saying no when we told her we would pick her up for church. After a first Sunday she had decided to tell us not to pick her up again. But when Pastor Bullis said, "I will pick you up next Sunday," she couldn't say no. Sundays passed and she attended regularly. In fact, she never missed a Sunday the first year, the second, and even the third.

At one point during all of those Sunday School lessons and church services, she came to know Christ as her Savior. It took more than the usual amount of courage for Mrs. Hazel Moore to come forward for baptism, but she did. The three years of perfect attendance grew into eleven.

How shall they hear without a preacher?

The Kolbs had allowed Mormons, Jehovah's Witnesses, and Armstrong groups to come to their home for a visit. Their Catholic background was very broad-minded. Pastor Bullis, who had come to know their Robbie in a park Bible School, was also allowed to come for a visit.

The message of salvation from the Scriptures was so true to the needs of their lives they both called upon the Lord for their salvation.

They came the next Sunday to see this odd group, not expecting it to be like the churches they had attended. They found these people and their worship strange. Yet, something kept attracting them, even though they didn't understand why—it was the difference. One Sunday morning, Gail stepped forth to say she had accepted Christ, and that she wanted to be a part of this group. David followed and their lives became one with the people. The Kolb family moved six miles from the church into a beautiful new home. They pledged it to the Lord.

They resided in Clarence, where we had conducted several park Bible Schools in the years before their move. David and Gail started a Bible study in their home. Finally, the day came when they chose to give up the security of Veteran's Park Baptist Church and start a new chapel in their living room. The Clarence Chapel was conceived due to their desire that others would know their Christ.

How can the message be proclaimed if the messengers do not go?

One evening we had fifty adults attend a mission dinner rally. They were from Veteran's Park, the mother church; Alden, our first chapel; and the Cheektowage and Batavia chapels. The purpose of this meeting was to say thank you for missions. Jim asked for testimonies from the people. The first was a woman who stepped forward and said, "Pastor Bullis, you came to the eastern side of Buffalo two years too late. My husband died without ever hearing how to get right. Why didn't you come sooner?"

How wonderful is the coming of the messengers?

In a dark, dingy living room sat a very old, very tired woman. Life had not treated her too well, and she had resorted to escape. It was a few drinks at first, but as time passed they increased since she had very little to live for. Along with the alcohol she was taking medicine, putting her in a life-threatening situation.

One evening the telephone rang. She made an effort to answer it and due to the patience of the caller, she did reach it in time.

The voice said, "Have you found it?"

She said, "I didn't know I'd lost it, but if I have, I would be glad to find it." As she listened, the voice on the telephone told her about Jesus and her need of him. When she was asked to pray the prayer, she prayed. Hanging up the receiver she was not sure what had happened. It was all so confusing. Why had this person called her?

Pastor Curtis Monday of our chapel took her card and in a few days knocked on her door. "Granny," as she is lovingly called, found a life worth living. She found a church family that has become her family.

What if they had never called? What if Granny had never found glad tidings of good things?

One evening Johnny was parked in his car at the shopping center. High on drugs with his head on his arm he said, "O God, if there is one, help me."

His attention was attracted by the form of the pastor coming across the parking lot, legs briskly walking, and lips whistling.

As he watched him he saw something else. Johnny, because of his bleary eyes, saw a light about the pastor's form.

Now, I am the first to know my husband had no angelic light about him, but I also know my Father is big enough to draw Johnny's attention to his messenger.

Without a word, Johnny drove to the church. The door was unlocked so he came in and spent time with the Lord.

One year before, the pastor had visited Johnny. He had heard the message of salvation, but only had laughed, along with the others in the room, who spoke from their viewpoints distorted by drugs.

Today Johnny has grown to the point where he eagerly leads Bible studies and is a sharer of glad tidings.

O Father, I thank you for the privilege of giving your message to those who have never heard. Hearing they believe and call upon Christ's name for salvation.

Your message is truly glad tidings—for them and for us.

19
───────Open House───────

"Come on in. I'd like to show you through the home of a pioneer mission pastor who serves on the extreme edge of the mission field. The houses are all different, and the faces of those who live in them are as different as snowflakes. Yet, on the outer edges where the work is hard and the people are unresponsive, the open house could be representative of most modern-day pioneer pastors.

"May I have your coats?

"Please step into our living room. Here you'll see the furniture which was purchased new when we were fresh out of seminary. Let me see . . . that was over eighteen years ago. At that time it was called "Danish Modern."

"Yes, you can sit on it. Our four boys have wrestled across its arms. We have replaced its cording and pads several times. I've covered the cushions three—no four—times. Oh, it needs covering again, but that can wait until next year.

"Where did I purchase the rugs? They came from a Holiday Inn where they were replaced by easier colors to keep clean. Very reasonable though. You say you'd hate them? Well, sometimes I would like . . . but then . . . they are rugs.

"Please come and stand in front of this painting. I wouldn't want you to miss its beauty. It is a semi-original painted on wallboard by "Starving Artist." If you're interested in a duplicate you can find them on street corners or in front of a gas station. Jim has often thought of replacing it, but I wouldn't hear of it, since it was one of our few anniversary gifts. You see, our anniversary is August 24. After the summer program of feeding so many workers and our family . . .

"I have plans for this room. When I get the time, I'll make new drapes, an afghan for the couch, and doilies for the tables. I love flowers and plan to purchase some when . . . I have time to water and care for them.

"Now into the dining room.

"I'd like to introduce you to this table. It is sixteen years old; also "Danish Modern." It came with one leaf but could hold three. I wouldn't let the salesman rest until he ordered the other two since we have as many as twelve or fourteen folks around this table during our summers.

"So you noticed the chairs? You guessed it. They were Danish Modern too, but our active family tested them for several years and they were dismantled piece by piece. We have replaced them with these ultrabeautiful, brown-painted, tubular-leg chairs. Note the wooden seats and the genuine autographs. You guessed it—they're chairs from a school. They came in a truckload of school furniture on which Jim received the lowest bid. They are sturdy!

"Sorry I can't show you my Danish Modern hutch. Somehow I couldn't afford one. Maybe in a few more years?

"You are interested in the dinnerware? That is the original pattern of the Early Mel-Mac. Would you believe these few pieces are all that remains of four sets of the gorgeous unbreakable dishes. There were never enough cups.

"The silverware? Oh, I'm sorry, it's not silver. You could tell? It seemed more important to have enough forks and knives for the summer crew.

"You're interested in seeing the upstairs? Come, I'll show you.

"This bedroom is made up entirely of barn furniture. Yes, I said barn furniture. There was a woman who had a barnful of old furniture. We picked up pieces to have extra for our summer workers, and kept what we liked or wasn't broken.

"You're interested in the old chest of drawers? Lovely, isn't it. Sorry it is not an antique . . . just well-used.

"Now into the second bedroom. Oh, yes, another room of barn furniture. This was the boys' bedroom. Originally we had two sets of bunks for the four boys. After the years passed and the boys grew, the bunks broke. Each time one of the four left home we could put together the best parts of the remaining bunks. This way we kept a "good bed" until we replaced them with these.

"The desk and the chair were discovered by the boys. They didn't say where they picked them up. The television is black and white.

"This is the third bedroom. No, this isn't barn furniture, as you can see. When Jim's mother died . . . we love this dearly since it is really all we have to remind us.

"Now down to the basement.

"Watch your step!

"Sorry it's so cluttered—Jim is a collector. He says it may be useful—I say it's junk.

"In this corner you'll find the washer and dryer. They are replaced about every three years. Hard on them? Yes. Where do we purchase them? We choose them carefully. When I call I ask only one question. It is not how old they are, but rather how many are in the family? If they have three children or more the appliance is not good enough. If they have only one child, I make them an offer.

"As we go back up from the basement, I want to remind you the house is equipped with the new furniture purchased eighteen years ago or its older replacements. When we retire, maybe we'll get a color TV, but first we must buy an antenna.

"Oh! You must leave? Let me get your coats.

"Thank you for coming. Please come again. Bye now!"

O Father, you did! . . . Not only make me happy, but satisfied!

God, Rock of our Foundation, may we hide in a small cleft when all breaks loose around us?

20
——— God's Protection ———

God of humor, can you help us through our imaginary fears?

Three things, yea, four I dislike. They are: Texas tornadoes, black widow spiders, tarantulas, and poisonous snakes. I was thankful to be in Western New York where none of these exist.

One summer my assurance faced a testing when a vocal summer missionary, protective of his young charges, saw a "very real copperhead" disappearing into the tall grass.

The unswerving certainty of this East Coast volunteer's report placed the camp on "snake alert." The campers were calmly informed that "no snakes are to be touched this summer." The counselors were privately warned of the possibility that a snake could have fallen from a passing railroad car on the tracks parallel to our land. A serpent could have entered our Eden!

I rushed to the drugstore, a second drugstore, and a third one to purchase a snakebite kit. The druggist accepted my order with a shrug and commented, "There are no poisonous snakes in Western New York. It'll be necessary to order it from one of our central distribution centers which should take a week or two." With a twisted little smile he added, "I'm sure your campers will be safe until it arrives."

I returned to camp with a definite sense of failure. Our counselors were prodded by the "Eastern expert" to remind the younger children that they were not to handle snakes. I gathered my kids together on the rows of the old theater seats beneath the big, forty-by-sixty, blue-and-white striped, circus tent. Perched on a heavy, wooden table with my feet barely touching the ground, I cautioned in my most dramatic voice:

"Children, do not touch a snake. If you see one, run in the other direction."

My lecture was interrupted by a child on the first row:

"Ms. Mary, look!"

"Where?"

"There is a snake going under your shoes!"

Even though I should be calm and not frighten the little ones, I had no control over my body. I jumped up on the table while shouting, "Like this children, get away from them like this!" I watched the slithering, serpentine figure as it crawled determinedly away.

I had certainly demonstrated my theory of "preventive withdrawal with deliberate haste" from the slender reptile which I now recognized as a little, green grass snake.

The snakebite kit came, only to gather dust in a forgotten corner. However, the cold winters which protected us from the snakes and insects did prove a danger to us.

For instance, take the blizzard of 1977 which covered Buffalo, putting all the area's inhabitants in danger.

God, can you watch over us when fear seems to be everywhere?

A church member's car had been placed in the shop for repairs, and we planned to give her a ride to work in the Northeastern side of Buffalo. The previous snow had piled like a feathered comforter across the land, and the cold temperature seemed to make the world an inviting place, as peaceful as a Currier and Ives Christmas card scene. We drove the seven miles with only one warning of the danger which lay ahead. The snow hadn't been cleared from the preceding night's fall on the secondary roads, and an icy sheet lay beneath the snow. A large truck came toward us, forcing Jim to pull to our extreme right and allowing our car to slip off into the ditch. Minutes later a pickup truck pulled us out, and we continued down the powdery, slippery road.

We headed home where Jim drove to check on the lady's car. When he returned, I told him he had better return to get her, because the "Blizzard of the Decade" was moving in.

As we traveled back to her place of employment, the snow was blowing horizontal to the ground. The wipers and heat of the car made a small hole through which we could see the world freezing solid. We had no trouble making the seven miles to pick her up, but then the blinding force of a dreaded "whiteout" was on us. The air was filled with snow.

"Lord, you know we slipped off this road earlier when we brought her to work. Can you aid us across this same dangerous land when we can no longer see ahead of us?"

We arrived at the six-lane road, the master artery, of the Northeast-Southeast traffic. We headed Southeast toward home. The speedometer read five miles an hour. We faced terrifying wind, throwing its heavy artillery at us. Every turn of the wheels seemed an act of futility. We couldn't make it home! Creeping along, we passed many cars abandoned in the middle of the street. We reached the bridge announcing the entrance to the New York Turnpike. Now we were halfway home. We crawled to a stop since the six-lane artery was completely plugged with trucks, cars, and vans. Huge trucks had tried to go off the road right-of-way and around the blockage only to be stuck. All wheels were now silent, and we sat in a world held together with the rhythm of powerful motors going nowhere.

There we sat in our second converted police car. It was a powerful machine with independent drive which allowed both rear wheels to pull at varied ratios. We stared at the road. The right showed an orphaned semi. In front was a van minus a driver, its motor silent. Just beyond was a lane still open where the traffic had gone around the original offender. Cars were piling up behind us.

Jim climbed and blinked at the freezing outside, his face tingling under the intense wind-chill factor. Soon he was joined by three men whose cars were trapped behind us. Together they decided our police car could push past the van barricade, but the bumpers didn't meet. The three men climbed on the hood of our car and shoved with their feet at the van's back door. Both vehicles moved on the ice. They called for Jim to start the motor, and our studded tires whined against the ice. Our helpers' legs pumped, and the van inched sideways, following the direction in which the steering wheel had been left. At last it nudged the semi on its right, creating a small passageway ahead. We backed up and moved free, followed by the other cars.

"Thank you, God, for we are moving!"

We drove down the empty road as the wind bitterly attacked our weaving car. We saw signs of the unseen, long hill between us and home. Knowing that the undercoating of ice would stop our car in the hill's upper incline, we turned west and away from home to avoid the hill.

We entered a side street in the general direction we wanted to go, allowing us some progress. At last we were two miles from home and ahead of us were flashing, red lights warning us of trouble. A policeman informed us that all roads were closed. We had to retrace our course, turning on the first road which would carry us in the direction of home. After a short distance we found it traversed by drifts caused from high winds and open industrial land. As we sat looking at a six-foot-high drift we knew we would remain in this spot since it was effectively dammed.

A small four-wheel-drive vehicle drove up. The driver honked his "celestial" horn and maneuvered past us to the front where he began attacking the drift with the tenacity of a Boston terrier. The weary drivers watched the small vehicle chew at the frozen mass. The waters began to part.

We cheered as the spunky little vehicle pushed away the last of the remaining mound, only to see the winds behind us at work, ferociously rebuilding their dike of snow. Again we were on our way.

We stopped at the church, drawn by its blazing lights. There were Barbara and Jack Wilson and Herm Clouse. They laughed as they paraded forth a succulent turkey which Barbara had brought to the day-care center for dinner the next day. They had called the police to share the news: the church doors were open for any who needed shelter or food during the night.

We knew they would have an exciting night at the church. We then headed into the last mile home. As we made a turn from the main street there was one last drift in our path. Jim recklessly slammed the car into the drift. Slowly the amazing Plymouth pulled back and attacked again. It was emulating its little brother, the jeep. Again . . . again . . . and at last we were home.

The trip was less than seven miles and yet had taken six hours. We had watched the frozen "rivers" part; "angels" had come to our rescue. We were given green lights amid the flourishing red lights of danger and approached the warmth of our home with thanksgiving. The hand of the Lord does protect.

God, you who know when we are in danger, can your voice of warning be heard?

The lesson of God's protection was taught by a bus that seemed to speak as Balaam's donkey warned its master. Two school buses had been parked in front of our house. Now they were being readied for the long trip to new owners. It was a retirement from the strenuous life of school transportation to more sedentary church life. Their seven-year-old bodies would serve to reach boys and girls for Christ.

Jim and I were supposed to deliver them. We would earn some needed commission to be used in the church program, share the special adventures of long hours on the road, and race back to make Sunday services at the church.

The buses had been checked out thoroughly. A rebuilt motor, plus a new core in the radiator, was sported by one of the buses. We left early Monday, planning to be back Wednesday, knowing if anything happened we would have until Sunday.

Driving the buses meant conversing by signals for turns, stops, or our special signals for "I love you" or "I'm sleepy." It meant two people trying to sing the same song while separated by a hundred feet of asphalt and behind the steering wheels. We made a good team, helping each other along the tedious miles to get those buses through. We were proud of our record.

Our two yellow tortoises crawled through rural New York and Pennsylvania and then entered the "Buckeye State" of Ohio. Ohio was the bridge between the Northeast and the South.

Suddenly! A turn signal, Jim's bus sought the gravel, his brake lights brightened. A cloud of steam sprang from the fender and played peek-a-boo from under the bus.

I parked my bus behind its wounded companion and found its hood up and Jim glaring at the gaping hole in the recently recored radiator. He was angry as he pointed at the shambles of his second-mile service. The fan blades and shaft had broken loose from the water pump and had wrecked the radiator.

"Mary, back my bus up. I don't want to lie in the water," he said, bathing himself in self-pity.

I started the motor and backed up until he signaled for me to stop. My foot slid to the brakes and pushed—the pedal went to the floor. I shouted:

"No brakes, Jim!"

"What? The radiator has nothing to do with the brakes!"

He stepped inside the bus and looked at the limp brake pedal lying sickly on the cold floor.

We raised our heads and looked down the highway. Ahead of us was a steep, long, curving road. The exit roads ahead in the Cleveland area would end with stop signs on busy thorough-fares. We thanked God for his using this aggravation to stop us before we reached disaster.

We happily replaced brakelines and the radiator right there on the shoulder of the road. A Highway patrolman shook his head at two laughing people working on what they called their "talking" bus. He couldn't understand the greatness of God's timing.

God, who protected from the red dragon, can you protect us from the fumes of flame?

As soon as we saw the old house we knew we'd have to cook with butane. The round, squat bottles were there to remind us we were tied to the ravenous appetite of the cooking stove which seemed to consume more than our family of seven. We were hesitant to fill the cavernous belly of the metal dispenser of bottled gas since it cost too much.

The bottle had used its last gas on a Saturday morning, and we had company coming for Sunday dinner. Jim called the gas company, and it was explained that we couldn't have delivery since we had called too late.

"May I pick up a bottle of gas?" Jim asked.

"Of course, come by and we'll help you load it." And they did.

He was glad to bring home the "firewood" for the dinner. He then went out to put the tubes on but didn't know what to loosen to place the copper tubes from the stove to the bottles. Everything seems to be tight except where a brass valve entered a brass seat. It seemed finger-tight and indicated to Jim that it had to be removed.

With the last twist of the valve, it shot from his hands into the vacant lot next to us. The gas screamed a crazy song of release alongside our house.

Jim yelled for me to get the children out of the house and to call the fire department from the gas station across the street. He rushed to the basement to pull the fuses, since there was a broken cellar window by the spewing tank. The threat of the pilot light in the oil furnace drove him from the house. The excitement grew as people came from all directions. The fire captain ordered the people to be kept back as we all anxiously waited for the house to explode.

But finally the house was declared safe The only reminder of the fearsome event was a small newspaper clipping simply stating that the fire department had responded to a call at the home of Rev. James Bullis. A butane bottle had discharged but no explosion resulted.

O Father, thank you for being the support of all our lives, and for providing a place of safety for us in times of danger.

The Lord who is still in his holy temple, who rules from heaven and watches all that happens here on earth, can you lead me through the valley of testing?

21
The Big End
—— of ——
the Stick

We stepped through the doorway of the hospital. I had been assured it would take only a short time, so I had packed just my robe, Bible, some balls of crochet yarn, and a toothbrush. I remembered telling my friends not to call or come since I would be right home.

The time would stretch into two weeks, and the card rack would overflow with hundreds of cards. There would be time for many visitors.

I, a red-haired mother of five red-haired children and foster mother of two brothers, was a busy pioneer pastor's wife. I knew I was loved, needed, and appreciated by my large family and our marvelous church family.

My husband of twenty-six years was a big, strong, kind, friendly man, also red-haired. We had shared many years of service for the Lord.

Our daughter had said, "My parents are not only husband and wife but friends." We do enjoy each other with a love and fellowship that is rare.

I found myself in a hospital room with a young woman of twenty-nine, who had suffered much from multiple sclerosis. As I prayed with her that night, my thoughts went to our strong, healthy family at home. I thanked the Father for his daily care and our good health.

The next day I told the nurses, doctor, and the world in general that I had no pain. There had been a few signs of blood. The very small amount of eight months earlier had increased as time passed.

The doctor had commented that it was probably polyps of the

intestines. I was only forty-five years of age, and cancer of the lower colon normally didn't develop until the fifties or later.

One of my greatest assets has been the ability to handle the rough spots in life, so I suffered all of the indignity of the barium X ray and was back in my room, happy that it was over and eager to go home.

My husband was there when the doctor came in with the X-ray results. He handed us the film and pointed out a napkin ring around my middle colon. He explained that it was a mature tumor of the sigmoid colon.

We looked and nervously smiled, waiting for the news of a simple cure. The doctor said it was important for us to understand what was wrong.

We informed him that we did understand that I had a tumor. My husband asked the question that was uppermost in our minds, "How many of the colon tumors are malignant?"

The doctor said, like a whiplash across our peace, "There are no nonmalignant colon tumors." I asked again, certain I had not heard correctly. It didn't change the second time he repeated it. My mind went blank. I simply sat and listened.

Later, my husband walked me down the hall to an empty office. I listened as he, a man of God that I trusted, prayed. He told God how much I was needed by him; how much I was needed by the boys; how much I was needed by our church family; how much I was needed in His service. As he prayed, he cried.

I asked him to leave me alone. He looked at me as he left and said, "If only I could kick a wall."

Back in my room I was now by myself, except for the Lord. My roommate had gone home to fight her battle. I lay quietly under my sheet, feeling small and let down. "Oh, Father, why?" I asked.

I opened my Bible and began to read. It had fallen open to Psalm 11. I had read just three stanzas when the Scriptures exploded into my dulled, unthinking mind.

It read:

> The Lord is still in his holy temple; he still rules from heaven. He closely watches everything that happens here on earth. He puts the righteous and the wicked to the test; . . . For God is good, and he loves goodness; the godly shall see his face" (Ps. 11:4-7, TLB).

I read it again and again. It said that the Father was watching over little me in that hospital bed. He whispered, "Mary, I see you, and I want you to know I am in control. I am great, and you will see my face in all that happens. I will test you, and you will know I am good."

I grabbed my pencil and underlined it in my Bible. My heart was so thankful. I had asked a question and the answer was there. I would be tested, yet in my heart I had a real peace.

Someone had contacted a Catholic priest to come up and help me in this time. Looking up I saw him at the door. He searched my face and said, "Have they finished your test?"

I replied, "Yes, sir, they have. I have a malignant tumor. It must be removed tomorrow. I gave my heart to Jesus when I was a child. My life has been his, and I know it will be all right." My voice was strong, but shakey.

I talked with him. "Oh, sir, life is abundant and full of joy in Christ. If I die tomorrow, I will go to be with him. I need nothing else done to me to get me there, and there is no in between. I will be with him."

I don't remember much the priest said as he went through the doorway.

I called my parents in Missouri. They assured me that they would be there to look after the boys. I was thankful since the foster children would also need someone to care for them. I took a piece of scrap paper and wrote a note to my church family. I told them I loved them and wanted to tell what the Father had done for me. I shared with them Psalm 11 and asked them to pray that I would pass the test.

Jim came back and said, "I have kicked my wall." He had gone to the Roswell Cancer Library and had looked up all they had on sigmoid colon cancers. This was like him. His sharp mind had devoured much in this short time. He wanted to be able to understand the doctors and to know the possible outcome.

Night brought the shots that would prepare me for sleep. I had a call from Brother Larry Kulcke some fifteen hundred miles away. He promised that their prayers would be with us. I was to hear later that calls like his had come from one end of the country to the other, each one promising to join the vigil of prayer.

I went to sleep that night, thanking the Father and knowing he did rule on the earth.

After surgery, the first people I saw were my mother and father. They had arrived from Missouri and were here to support me when I needed them. Jim was in and out during the day.

During the day I found I was at peace and had surprising strength. I could move around on the bed, and I had very little pain. As the days passed, this was even more apparent.

One night I prayed,

O Father, who lives on high and knows everything on the earth, the Father that brings all people to a test, only you could look down on me in intensive care and carry my pain. You always have carried the big end of the stick. Thank you, Father!

22
The
————Computer's————
Choice?

Two copies of the papers were handed to us to read while we sat in the small office of the hospital. Jim read his copy and sat in silence as I studied each word of mine.

My hands were a little shaky. My voice would not cooperate. The woman behind the desk excused herself and stepped from the room.

Jim finally spoke, "Mary, do you understand what it's saying?"

"Yes," I replied.

"Do you think we should sign?"

Again I said, "Yes."

After a few moments of getting myself together, I said, "This hospital should have my body if I die. It might help someone else to live." Jim read parts of the paper aloud to me. I took the pen and signed my name, Mary A. Bullis, Jim then signed on the line below.

Five weeks had slipped past since I had been hospitalized. It was now necessary to enter the Roswell Cancer Hospital for further testing to determine future treatments.

I was thankful this splendid cancer hospital was near where we lived. It is one of the best in the world. During our years of our ministry, we had known very few medical doctors. In fact, we have known only one cancer specialist.

God had worked out the needs ahead of time. This doctor was head of the colon department of the Roswell Hospital. He was Dr. James Evans, a member of one of our Southern Baptist churches. He was not only a doctor, but a Christian and a concerned friend.

If you put into a computer the possibility of our knowing a Christian doctor who was a colon specialist (which I needed), I am sure the computer would come up with a negative probability.

Dr. Evans arranged for my admittance. The tests were started early the next morning and continued during the day. A review of all surgical records and tests were to determine treatment.

A diagnostic technician came to explain the procedure. "There are four treatments. One will be chosen for you," she explained. "They include: no therapy but regular clinical visits, chemotherapy, fifty shots in the back, five at a time, or a combination of shots and chemotherapy."

She added, "Mrs. Bullis, do you understand the treatments and do you have any questions?"

"Yes," I said, "how will the treatment be decided?"

The technician answered, "We'll take your medical history, your surgical history, the results of all other tests, and information. Then we'll put them into a computer. The computer will feed back one of the treatments."

She paused, looked at me for a moment, and then asked, "How do you feel about a computer deciding your treatment?"

I smiled and wondered if she would understand what I was going to say to her, "God, who looks closely down on this earth, who knows everything that is happening, who brings the righteous and the unrighteous to a test, also knows what should go into the computer to provide the proper treatment. Since he is in control of the computer and also my body, I will accept whatever the computer feeds out."

The technician said, "You are a born-again believer. I'm glad. It makes my job so much easier knowing you trust God's will for your life."

Time went by quickly. Jim was busy during the day. He would either come early to take me home, or spend the evening with me if necessary to begin treatment.

I watched eagerly for the return of the technician. The door opened, but my friend Dr. Evans entered the room. He dropped into the chair by my bed as if the day had been too much for him.

He asked, "Did the technician come by to give you the results?"

"No," I replied.

He simply sat there without saying a word.

I knew what he was going to say. The doctors at the hospital had prepared me for chemotherapy. It would mean I would have to slow down. My body would be weakened while my lips, stomach, and possibly my hair would receive the worst effects.

I braced myself for the words I would hear from my doctor's lips. He said nothing. Without eagerness I asked, "Aren't you going to tell me? Don't make me wait on someone else. Tell me now."

His facial expression didn't change as he spoke only one word, "Nothing."

"What do you mean 'nothing'? Do you mean there will be no treatments?"

"Mary, no doctor on this earth can say if you need chemotherapy. You are a busy person, and I wouldn't want to put you through treatments unless it is absolutely necessary."

As he left the room I thought, *No doctor knows, but my Heavenly Father does. He works the computer which prescribed the treatment.*

I called home excitedly, "Jim, I am coming home. I won't have to come back for treatments. They'll watch my progress through clinic visits. I am ready to come home."

While I waited for Jim to come, I recalled the Sunday School lesson I had taught the young people; Hezekiah had prayed: "I beseech thee, O Lord, remember now how I have walked before thee in truth and with a perfect heart, and have done that which is good in thy sight." Tears had flooded King Hezekiah's eyes as he faced the wall and wept (2 Kings 20:3).

The prophet Isaiah returned to King Hezekiah and gave the message that the king he would be given fifteen more years.

I had prayed before surgery, "Oh, Father, I am ready to go and be with you, but there is still so much I want to see. Father, when I held each of our five children at their birth, I gave them to you. They still think they are in control of their futures, but I know you are fashioning a design for each of their lives. I want to see what you will make of them.

"I want to see our three chapels strengthened and see our church become grandmother and great-grandmother to many more new chapels. Jim needs my help. Together we will find a new city where new chapels can be born."

Jim arrived to take me home to begin my first year.
My prayer still is:

Please, Father, give me fifteen more years as you did Hezekiah so my eyes can see the desires of my heart become a reality. Amen and amen.

Lord God, who showed Israel the ease of crossing the impossible Red Sea, can you keep the flood tides from engulfing me?

23
——The Crossing Over——

In August, 1979, we took a lazy trip into Canada. Traveling up the Queen Elizabeth Highway we were introduced to the Golden Horseshoe area of Ontario. This region curves around the western portion of Lake Ontario. Its cities are like a chain of pearls, with the largest one being Toronto. The next city is Mississauga, then Burlington, and across the Burlington Bay is Hamilton. On to Saint Catherine's followed by the honeymoon capital of the world, Niagara Falls, and finally we arrived back in the United States.

Crossing into the homeland, our eyes looked back toward the land which was "pioneer" to Southern Baptists. We prayed, "Oh, Father, we would love to cross over." We waited to see if God would close the door or give us the freedom to enter.

Jim said, "I wish we could meet one Baptist who could help us locate the first chapel, but that is impossible."

Before the week was over our telephone rang. The call was from Byron Lutz, pastor of the inner-city church in Buffalo. He was the only pastor who knew of our desire to go northward. Brother Lutz asked if we were still interested in going to Canada. I eagerly replied, "Oh, yes."

"Would you like to meet a Baptist couple from Canada?" We were invited to Byron's home the next day to have lunch with the couple who had worked in Toronto for years.

They invited us to their home outside of Toronto. Jim and his new friend searched the maps, charts of the population, and digests of churches.

Jim asked, "Where is the best place to start a Southern Baptist chapel?"

Our friend suggested we go to Burlington; it is the hub of the Golden Horseshoe area. From it we could reach down to Hamilton and further east to Mississauga and Toronto and west to Guelph and Kitchener.

What had brought this couple to the home of Brother Lutz? A mail strike. A letter was to be mailed from the Home Mission Board of the Southern Baptist Convention. To assure its prompt delivery, they had mailed it to Brother Lutz in the United States and asked him to see to it that Jim received it. How wonderful it was sent to the only man who knew we wanted to go to Canada!

To us it seemed that God was not only directing us to Ontario, Canada, but pointing to the place of our beginning. We made many trips to Burlington before we moved on July 4, 1979.

During one of these visits we rented an apartment and a school meeting site. On the return trip Jim was driving leisurely up a country road, enjoying the sights of the new country. I was napping and didn't see the tandem dump truck making a left turn into our path. The effort to stop the car brought me to attention. I saw the green light but knew we couldn't avoid an accident. We hit the large front tire, causing our small car to bounce back violently instead of being crammed under the vehicle. We were not injured except for a broken bone in Jim's foot and my concussion which would have to travel its colorful course.

Four days later some of our friends at Veterans Park Baptist Church helped the Bullis boys load the large rental truck and pickup for our move. Every box had to be numbered and the contents listed in triplicate. The serial numbers on appliances were also noted. The pickup truck was loaded with 5,000 portions of Luke-Acts and 1,000 TEV New Testaments provided by the Home Mission Board.

Our application for visa had been completed many months before, but due to my cancer they couldn't rush the process. July 4 arrived before the legal paperwork was finished which would grant us permission to come as landed immigrants.

Jim had called the border customs office to ask if we would be permitted to cross before becoming landed immigrants. We were told it would be up to the border guard to allow us in as visitors. Two summer workers, two church members, and our family of four arrived at the Peace Bridge. We resembled a group on a church picnic.

The border guard was huge and rough-looking, and his voice was gruff and demanding. His message was, return to your place of origin. We found his attitude unusual since, later, all others have been kind.

After much explaining we did not have proper papers, but we had been told we would be allowed to come, we were at a dead end. The question from the man kept booming at us. "Who said you could come across? What was his name?" Who said? . . . "

At last we were invited into the office to see if our names were on a list for people allowed to cross for the Fourth of July. He explained this was a holiday and the immigration offices were closed. There was no way he could confirm that they looked favorable on our entry.

In the office he asked, "What is your name?" Jim said, "James Bullis." I interrupted and said, "Rev. James Bullis."

The look on the man's face changed. "Oh, you are a Reverend?" I must admit we didn't look the part. Jim had a cast on his leg, and I had two large, black eyes from the accident. At this point, the man at the border changed his tone. A young man at his side began making out our papers. I breathed a sigh of relief and returned to the others to give word I was sure it would all work out.

We were given permission to go ahead in the truck and pickup. Jim remained to do the paperwork. Later, we unloaded everything from the vehicles but Jim had not arrived. The hours passed and still no Jim.

We drove back to the border gate, but he was not there. Returning to the apartment, we found a message from our landlady saying that Jim's transmission had quit. He was at a station twenty miles away.

This red "junker" had been purchased to meet immediate transportation needs. When we found Jim and the two ladies who had come to help me, they were tired and hungry. Jim had pushed the car, struggling alone on his cast, to get the car to the station. His four-day-old cast was broken.

What a day! That night, I might have doubted the will of the Father if he had not made his will so clear before our crossing.

Crossing brought other problems.

Every time the Home Mission Board has crossed into pioneer areas, someone must go first. Before Ohio was recognized as a field, someone needed to fill a need.

The Southern Baptist Convention did not recognize the New York area when Rev. Zig Burrough came from Alabama.

No Southern Baptist Convention aid was approved for Western Canada when men crossed over from Washington-Oregon. Always someone opens the door before support can be granted.

For this reason we approached the Ohio State Baptist Convention to ask their assistance. Ray Roberts, then executive secretary, promised his support. The director of missions of the Capital City Association, Charles Magruder, sought sponsorship from that association. He also asked aid from Highland Baptist Church of Grove City as our mother church. All three sources came through.

Pastor Glen Stern and the Highland Baptist Church have extended support to us, making the adjustment easier. We couldn't have had a greater mother church.

Friends from the South became our financial supporters. First Baptist Church of Bernice, Louisiana, and small Camp Creek Baptist Church joined other Ohio churches to help make our salary and the rent on the school meeting place. Former summer missionaries and old friends became our life-support system into Canada.

After the crossing over, we had thirty days to get a congregation to attend our first service in the rented school. We knew no one in Burlington.

Jim started his door-to-door visits. He hobbled along on his crutch. I knew I should help him, but I looked at myself in the mirror and realized I looked like a raccoon. My eyes were black, and one front tooth was broken.

I found some pan-cake makeup and carefully placed it over the black of my eyes. I spread it over the blue-green which had crept down into my cheeks.

Satisfied, I went out the door. I faced a neighborhood boy who had become my friend. I said, "Keith, can you see my black eyes?"

He looked long and hard, and then he said, "No, Ma'am." I smiled and thought I was no longer a raccoon's cousin. Then he said, "I can sure see that gook you have on your face." I was not sure which would look best, the gook or the black eyes.

Three missionaries came from the states to help us prepare for our first service. We had our first Bible School in the park near our apartment and visited door to door around the school we had rented.

How beautiful were the twelve Canadians, one summer missionary, and our family of three who attended the first Southern Baptist worship service in Burlington!

O Father, who brought Israel across the Red Sea and helped her take the Promised Land, thank you for letting us cross over to the beautiful promised land of Canada.

My Savior, who prayed, "Thy will be done," help me to share your will with others.

24
———Thy Will Be Done———

It had been two-and-a-half years since I entered the world of cancer.

We arrived home August 15, 1980, from a visit with our children in Fort Worth, Texas, following a World Missions Conference. We had become concerned about my health since my waist had increased two inches during the two weeks.

My weight and waist had also grown during the preceding summer. We had guests from Ohio, Bermuda, and Louisiana to cook for. They had come to visit our field. I had also prepared five meals for the two choir groups which had worked in our Bible Schools. After noticing the gain, I had become diet-conscious and had started walking two miles each day.

Every evening of the World Missions Conference in Monroe I was more self-conscious. It looked as if I were seven-months pregnant.

Jim would have rushed to buy diapers if it had not been for the negative results of the pregnancy test he had insisted on purchasing.

Monday morning we reported to the Roswell Cancer Hospital and drove back and forth daily until Thursday. By Wednesday they determined I had a large abdominal mass. A new doctor friend explained I had an 85 percent chance they could do surgery. They hoped to remove the problem area which was suspected to be an ovary or the uterus. He was positive other areas were involved.

After we left the hospital, tears exploded down my cheeks. Jim, in his frustration, made a wrong turn. We entered streets in Buffalo which were unfamiliar to us. I tried to strangle each stubborn sob. They betrayed my feelings. Jim halted at a stop sign. Looking out the window to avoid Jim's look of helplessness, I saw my message from God. It was a large billboard. I began to laugh. It was so like my Father to place before my eyes his promise. I read the sign aloud to Jim: "You can still trust in God."

In Canada I said, "Jim, I know God would not have let us come to Canada if he were not going to give us time to start Southern Baptist churches in Hamilton and other cities. I can still trust in God."

On Thursday I was admitted to the hospital for eight days of tests. I walked the halls, visited patients, and shared my faith with many between tests.

In the room next to me was Agie. Her coming surgery was planned to give her a year. Cancer had ravished her body. Her response to my visit was, "Well, we all love 'Mother Mary' even though we are of different religions."

"Agie, I do not worship Mary. She was the mother of Jesus. I love and serve Jesus, because he is the one who died for my sins."

She listened closely as I continued sharing with her how I had trusted Jesus as a child and how he had guided me through all of life.

Every evening I built a worship time in her room. I shared with the Father and her my desire for her to come to know his love and peace.

The night before her surgery I said, "Agie, I am going to pray a prayer and if you will it squeeze my hand." I started, "Oh, Father, my friend Agie needs you as her Savior. She has sinned and needs your forgiveness. Your Spirit must come to be her helper since she has a long battle to fight. Please, Lord Jesus, come and be Agie's Master." Agie squeezed my hand and would not let go.

Agie went for surgery and was in intensive care. I went to see her when she returned. My surgery was past and I had been given an unusual recovery.

Her faint voice said, "Mary, I am so sick I wish I had died."

"Oh, Agie, I know you are. You are weak. You can hardly breathe, let alone fight. But Agie, God wants you to live, or you would have died. He wants you to live to tell your friends that Christ is your Lord and Master. Let's talk to him about it."

Again I prayed as I held her frail hand, "Oh, Father, my friend Agie is so weak. She cannot fight. She belongs to you."

Her hand managed a squeeze.

I continued, "Father, I pray that you will share your strength. Help her to claim the impossible and get better. Only you can bring victory over her weakness. May you surround her with your love and care."

During a later visit I found Agie was doing well. She said, "Mary, I read the Bible you gave me every day."

I had become increasingly aware of the *Watchtower* and the healing magazines which were everywhere—but no Bibles.

I was led to a sweet black lady whose biweekly craft cart visits covered the hospital. Eagerly I asked, "Would you make available on your craft cart some *Good News for Modern Man*? I could provide them through the Home Missions Board of the Southern Baptist Convention."

"Honey," she answered, "if I have room for anything on my cart, I have room for God's Word."

Two cases of the testaments were given to her. The Southern Baptist associational missions director's name and phone number were written in them so we could extend a helping hand.

On Friday morning I was taken to surgery. By four in the afternoon I was returned to my room. Jim came in to tell me they had removed a large tumor. It was malignant. They had also removed a "cyst."

My stay in bed was one of the shortest they had seen. No pain or problems made it possible for all support systems to be removed by Tuesday. This gave me four days to visit my sick friends.

A middle-aged man pointed out one of the *Good News* Bibles which I had left in the waiting room. He said, "I woke up three times during the night and made my way here to read this book. I could not put it down. It is the most interesting book I have ever read."

Early my last morning I made my way to another waiting room. A tall, thin man came in and sat down. I said, extending him my *Good News Bible* in which I had been reading, "I would like to give you this. The first four books are Matthew, Mark, Luke, and John. They tell about Jesus."

The man pointed toward the waiting-room library to the one book among fifty other books. I had placed it there the night before. "There's one just like it," he said.

"Yes," I said, "I put it there, but I want you to have this copy for your own. In the third chapter of John you will find the story of a great

Jewish leader who came to Jesus. Jesus told him he must be born again. This Jewish man said, 'I can't be born again. How can I enter into my mother's womb and be born again?' Jesus said, There are two births, one physical and the other spiritual."

The tall man stopped me and said, "When I came here, they asked me if I wanted to see a rabbi. I told them I had rather see a priest since my wife is Catholic. I had a good talk with the priest."

This idea of his being a Jew was new to me. I continued, "Nicodemus was a great Jewish leader—still Jesus said he must be born again. Another great Jewish leader was named Saul. While on the road to Damascus to kill the Christians, a bright light shone, and Saul fell to the ground. God's voice spoke, and Saul knew it was God. God said, 'Why don't you stop tearing up what I am doing?'" I told him more of the man named Saul who became Paul, the great missionary.

I said, "Friend, Jesus doesn't force himself on you as a Jew or on me as a Gentile. But he knocks at your heart's door. He knocks through people like me. I didn't plan to be here this morning to tell you this. God put me here."

Nodding his head, my friend said, "The last time I was at home a man told me the same thing. But, I wouldn't listen because he kept saying, 'When you die, you will want to go to heaven.' I did not want to think of dying. I wanted to live."

With a smile I said, "The man had not walked in our shoes. I want to live also. I fight to live, but my fight is made easier by Jesus. I am offering you a Friend who can help you fight to live, but who can give you a peace in knowing that when the fight is over you will be with him."

The man left the room with the *Good News Bible* deep in the pocket of his robe. He was to have surgery on his liver.

On Friday, one week after my surgery, I asked my doctor for more information about the cyst.

He said, "I cannot tell you about the cyst since I know nothing about it. Your body is unusual, and we don't understand it. There were five doctors present during the surgery, and none of us had ever seen a cyst like yours. We call it 'Mary's cyst' for lack of a better name."

"Doctor, I'm ready to go home. When can I go?" was my next question.

"If I let you go home tomorrow, you will be home in time to go to church to hear your husband preach, won't you?"

"Yes, and that's just what I'll do."

My papers were signed for my release Saturday morning.

Ten days later the unfamiliar cyst was explained to us. The doctor drew a picture of the enlarged ovary, which had weighed over five pounds. Then he drew a picture of the cyst surrounding it. It was as if God had placed the malignant tumor in a bag. The cyst's inner lining had been affected. The three fourths of a gallon of fluid in the cyst, and the outer lining surrounding the organs of my body, were negative.

Jim said, "Doctor, what percent of ovary tumors have such a cyst?" The doctor replied, "There is no percent. The information we have was discovered in medical journals. A doctor would not expect to see it more than once in a lifetime."

God had prevented the malignant ovary from spreading throughout my body. Jim and I smiled as the words "You can still trust in God," flooded our thoughts.

I was scheduled for chemotherapy in six weeks. The doctors prepared me for the ensuing weakness, plus the discomfort of the treatment.

A new doctor was placed in charge of the chemotherapy treatments. He asked to speak with my doctor. They were away some twenty minutes. When they returned, the new doctor said, "I do not feel you need chemotherapy. No malignancies are apparent in your body at this time. We will keep a close check on you, and if some appear we will take care of them at that time."

We left the hospital highly elated. God was so good.

I recalled only seven weeks earlier a lady sitting across from me in our living room. She said, "Mary, you are wrong. You should claim God's healing."

I said, "No doctor has ever said I am healed. I would not want to make God a liar. I claim only one thing." With strong confidence I said, "I claim God is in control of my body."

Jesus on his knees in the garden knew the agony of his death. He prayed to his Heavenly Father. "Father, . . . All things are possible for you. Take this cup of suffering away from me. Yet, not what I want, but what you want" (Mark 14:36, TEV).

I know my Heavenly Father can do all things. He can take all the cancer away from me. Yet, it must not be what I want, but it must be his will.

O Father, you are in control of every tiny cell of my body. May your will be done.

Epilogue

My father, also deacon and pastor, Arnold Epps had bathed us in his love and concern. The letter inviting us to come home to an ordinary church is one of my richest memories. Yet, others have wondered why my husband and I have bypassed the time-proven, great churches of the South and Southwest. Why should we go to places where people have never heard?

Jim and I were visiting in a town house when a prospect cheerfully said, "Work hard and see this church grow, and you will probably be offered a 'real church.'"

We were invited back to the tenth anniversary of the Veteran's Park Baptist Church. Over 200 people gathered for the morning or afternoon services. Many people from churches or chapels came by to say, "Because you came we learned of the saving power of Jesus Christ." These had been the proof of our ministry. This is a once-in-a-lifetime joy when one is surrounded by precious grain, harvested and winnowed.

We saw these as the Lord's unusual servants. Some came from every background and educational level. Yet they were a family from whom Jim and I could always draw strength. Recently they had elected us as their missionaries-at-large. We had touched the smallest tip of an iceberg, and it had begun to thaw. No cost can compare with the grace of their lives.

Jim Sinclair tells of reading the Oklahoma Baptist state paper and finding an article. It was by a pastor who "waxed eloquent" as he wrote, "From New York to California; from Mexico to Canada our people will share the great light." This native Canadian, who loves

Southern Baptists, wrote in return, "Why stop at a border or let a dream die at a lake? Come all the way over to Canada and start your churches here."

Upon hearing of our coming, this man who loves Southern Baptists wrote, "I have prayed for years the churches of the Southern Baptist Convention would share the dreams of our Baptist churches which already labor here. You have much to offer."

Each time Jim and I cross the border the immigration officers stop us and ask, "Where do you live?"

"Burlington, Canada," is our answer.

"Are you Canadian citizens or landed immigrants?"

"No," we reply.

"Why are you driving a Canadian car and living in Canada?"

"I have cancer and cannot be a permanent part of Canada. We are visitors."

Day by day and month by month, without any other right than the kindness of the Canadian government, we remain as visitors, until my FATHER calls me home.

> I am a stranger here, within a foreign land;
> My home is far away, upon a golden strand.
> . . . .
> My home is brighter far than Sharon's rosy plain,
> Eternal life and joy thro'out its vast domain;
> My Sov'reign bids me tell how mortals there may dwell,
> And that's my business for my King.
>
> This is the message that I bring,
> A message angels fain would sing:
> "Oh, be ye reconciled,"
> Thus saith my Lord and King,
> "Oh, be ye reconciled to God."
>
> "The King's Business"—E. Taylor Cassel